PERFECTLY GOLDEN

gluten-free
when it matters

vegan if you like

dairy-free
if you need

PERFECTLY GOLDEN

Adaptable Recipes for Sweet and Simple Treats

ANGELA GARBACZ

Owner, Goldenrod Pastries

PHOTOGRAPHS BY DANIEL MULLER

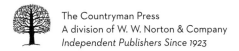

The Countryman Press
A division of W. W. Norton & Company
Independent Publishers Since 1923

For information about permission to reproduce selections from this
book, write to Permissions, The Countryman Press, 500 Fifth Avenue,
New York, NY 10110

For information about special discounts for bulk purchases, please
contact W. W. Norton Special Sales at specialsales@wwnorton.com
or 800-233-4830

Manufacturing by Versa Press
Book design by Nick Caruso Design
Production manager: Devon Zahn

Library of Congress Cataloging-in-Publication Data

Names: Garbacz, Angela, author.
Title: Perfectly golden : adaptable recipes for sweet and simple treats /
    Angela Garbacz, Owner, Goldenrod Pastries.
Description: New York, NY : The Countryman Press, a division of
    W. W. Norton & Company, Independent Publishers since 1923,
    2020. | Includes index.
Identifiers: LCCN 2020002620 | ISBN 9781682684764 (cloth) | ISBN
    9781682684771 (epub)
Subjects: LCSH: Baking. | Desserts. | LCGFT: Cookbooks.
Classification: LCC TX773 .G338 2020 | DDC 641.81/5—dc23
LC record available at https://lccn.loc.gov/2020002620

The Countryman Press
www.countrymanpress.com

A division of W. W. Norton & Company, Inc.
500 Fifth Avenue, New York, NY 10110
www.wwnorton.com

10 9 8 7 6 5 4 3 2 1

For my grandmothers,
Helen Dow Cariotto and Katarzyna Pawęska Garbacz.

This book is dedicated to the women I work with
at Goldenrod. May your minds always be filled with the
sound of one another's laughter.

CONTENTS

BUNS + YEASTED TREATS

46

COOKIES

74

INTRODUCTION
Welcome to Goldenrod Pastries

LIFE AT GOLDENROD PASTRIES It's a Tuesday at 1 p.m. at Goldenrod Pastries. I'm sitting at the counter, looking into our open kitchen. I'm surrounded by loaves of banana bread topped with walnuts and sesame seeds, stacked round pans of walnut and almond crusts ready to be filled with cheesecake batter, a half-full pan of my grandma's famous peach coffee cake, a few caramel-covered pecan rolls with caramel-coated pecans falling off the sides of each roll, and containers of multicolored, pastel sprinkles, waiting to be chosen for custom cakes, cookies, and pound cakes.

But the most wonderful things I can see are my coworkers buzzing around the kitchen. We are going into a holiday week and there's no shortage of work to do. The relatively small countertop mixer is in constant rotation; one baker is using it and another is on deck to use it right after she is done. The food processor has been grating zucchini for the past hour—our regular customers are excited that our Zucchini Chocolate Cake (page 122) is back for as long as our farmer has zucchini. We are finalizing a new line of bun-inspired merchandise to sell in the store. The front door keeps opening with a constant stream of people,

refrigerator doors are closing, just in time for another bakery babe to slip right by. Pink pastry boxes are being folded, stuffed with gently wrapped pieces of cardamom pound cake, confetti cookies, and gorgeous lemon poppy seed muffins. The pink boxes are shut, sealed with a Goldenrod sticker, and sent out the door with all of our favorite regular customers. We work in tight quarters, and during a busy week like this, we all reach a state of flow, something I love to be a part of and love to watch.

Goldenrod Pastries is absolutely buzzing. It's my favorite kind of day here. It's the kind of day I imagined I would have every single day when I imagined having a bakery, which I did imagine for a very long time.

At age five, I started watching food television. Emeril Lagasse started his trademark *BAM!* and taught America the best way to cut onions. It didn't take more than a few minutes for me to pull up a chair to the kitchen island and start teaching myself to cut onions and mimicking the *BAM!* movement on everything I ate, drank, or came in contact with. My best friend Ashley and I started our own cooking show, with a giant VHS video recorder propped on the kitchen counter, imagining that we were the next big female food television duo, right after Mary Sue Milliken and Susan Feniger of *Too Hot Tamales* fame. We played off each other, told jokes, and talked about our favorite foods. My favorite activity, cooking, was now something being shown to me as a career. It made me wonder what could be out there waiting for me.

Dessert was always a mainstay in our house while I was growing up—it was neither feared or praised. If we wanted to make chocolate chip cookies before bed at nine o'clock at night, that's what we did: my brother Andy, sister Betsy, and I crowded around the stand mixer with my mom at the helm. She never told us to stop eating the cookie dough, or that we'd had enough of any one thing. We ate cookies to our hearts' content, with pure joy every time. My dad coined the term "donut diplomacy" when he started taking donuts, and eventually other pastries, to meetings. "You can buy a lot of goodwill with a dozen donuts," he told us.

At the end of middle school, I started my first job at a small, local grocery store where I would weigh fruits and vegetables for customers, marking the total price on paper bags with ink pencils. This grocery store drew in professors, world travelers, and people who had immigrated to the United States and landed in Lincoln, Nebraska. I listened to my customers' stories of where they traveled, what they ate, and what they were going to make at home. I learned that you could make Italian prune-plum cakes with cornmeal and almond flour, and that in some parts of the world, people were poaching pears in red wine. I knew I had to keep working in food, so I looked for a job in a kitchen.

After a short stint at a local bakery where my coworker and I ate massive amounts of sprinkles and frosting, I landed in the pastry kitchen in the restaurant at a golf course. The chef I worked for could see that I wanted to learn more than

just my dessert station on the dinner service line. He taught me a new technique every day and would test me on it the next day. He started by teaching me the five mother sauces one day, and quizzing me on them the next day. I was hooked.

When it came time for college, I stayed in town and started earning my bachelor's degree in culinary and food sciences at the University of Nebraska-Lincoln. At the same time, I ran the pastry department at a brand-new French bakery in town, owned by two brothers. I loved to work and looked forward to rushing out of class, skidding off campus, and getting to the bakery as fast as I could. We spent so much time together, working long overnight shifts, that they felt like family. The food community seemed to be shifting in Lincoln—the main-stays and chains would stick around, but now there were new opportunities to branch out. I was really hopeful that, with the right experience, I could help to create one of these opportunities. In my quest to learn more about pastries and the food industry in general, I took a break from my studies at the University of Nebraska to attend the French Culinary Institute, now called International Culinary Center, in New York City in 2008. With its Classic Pastry Arts program lasting only six months, I knew my time there was short, so I worked every minute I wasn't in class. I had an internship at school in culinary technology. I worked for Dave Arnold, who became one of my greatest mentors and was an incredible example of leadership in the food industry. I met some of my closest friends during that internship. (Hello to Mindy, Nick, and Peder—and our dear Eng Su, who we lost in September 2019.) On the days I didn't work at school, I rushed uptown to work in one of New York's finest pastry kitchens. I kept my head down and worked, hoping to catch the attention of the executive pastry chef. When the other interns were tired and went home, I asked for more projects. I remember the moment specifically when I offered to fill macarons after another intern had left and Alina, the most graceful and focused pastry chef I've ever seen, noticed that I stayed and thanked me. I worked with incredible people in that kitchen.

I thought I wanted to stay in New York forever to work as a pastry chef and have my own bakery. With the ultimate childhood dream of opening a bakery, I knew in my heart that I needed to return to my roots in Nebraska to invest in the community and open the bakery there. I returned to Lincoln to finish my time at the university and earn my degree.

The more time I spent in my hometown, the more I realized how special our community is. I started working in international marketing, met my husband, Russell, who also is a trained chef and educated food scientist, and made food for as many people as I could in my free time. My apartment's galley kitchen was always covered in cakes and cookies and buns. If I wasn't baking for an order, I took every-thing I had baked to work. I packed myself little slices of cake and stacks of cookies to enjoy throughout the days. I baked nonstop, always trying to tempt people into my world with pastries. It was donut diplomacy again in my adult world.

STARTING GOLDENROD PASTRIES

During this time, I discovered that I had a dairy allergy. I decided to start a blog, which I called *Goldenrod Pastries* after the state flower of Nebraska. In it, I chronicled my journey learning how to bake dairy-free desserts for myself. I was nervous about sharing my blog publicly, but felt it was necessary for the next step in my career. Despite wondering whether people would think I was vain for sharing my anecdotes and recipes, I did it, and within about a month of publishing it online, orders came rolling in: people were looking for pastries—donuts, birthday cakes, cookies, and tarts— that were dairy-free, gluten-free, vegan, and every combination of those.

With my full-time job in marketing, I was baking before and after work, every weekend, and running to make pastry deliveries during my lunch hour. I booked weddings and sold at small market stands. I baked for birthdays, anniversaries, and for people just craving cinnamon rolls. After four months, I realized it was time to open a brick-and-mortar bakery. And only a year after I posted my blog publicly, Goldenrod Pastries opened. We served more than 1,200 customers during our four-hour grand opening.

During the blogging workshop I attended in 2014, one of the teachers said, "You can be whoever you want to be. It doesn't matter who you've been in the past, who people think you are, or who they expect you to be. You can start over whenever you want and be whoever you want." And with my bakery opening, I had entered a new chapter of my life, and had reinvented myself and found my strength and my voice in the process. The kitchen is the one place I have always felt like myself and have felt confident and proud. Goldenrod Pastries was a turning point for me in many ways. I decided that the person I wanted to be was someone who shared her stories, her recipes, and her experiences. In the back of my mind, I heard all of the women who had bullied me most of my life, I thought about the times I didn't fit in, and remembered ex-boyfriends who told me I was "dull and uninspiring" and "never going anywhere," and I said, "This won't be my story."

GOLDENROD PASTRIES IS BORN

During the period of time I was blogging and baking from my home kitchen, the most common questions I heard were about cakes and other treats for people with food allergies or sensitivities. I couldn't be the person who said no to making a birthday cake, especially for someone who hadn't been able to have one for years, due to dietary restrictions. So, I learned how to make gluten-free and vegan cakes, in addition to the dairy-

BEVERAGES

CULTIVA COFFEE 3
ICED TODDY 3
TEA 2.75
MILK 1.50
LA CROIX 1
MATCHA 4
LAVENDER LEMONADE 4

BUNS

TUE   PECAN ROLLS
WED   CARDAMON TWISTS
THUR   FLUFFER NUTTER
FRI
&   BAKERS CHOICE
SAT

BUNS
BUN
BUNS

free pastries I was already learning how to make. I knew that Goldenrod Pastries had to be a place where we could make birthday cakes for as many customers as possible. I wanted to learn how to make cakes and cookies that were safe to eat for people who need to follow a specific diet, but delicious for everyone to eat. I wasn't going to settle for pastries that were "good for gluten-free"—they had to be delicious pastries, regardless of the ingredients. Five years later, I am proud to say that while we do have a large number of customers who do need to eat dairy- or gluten-free, many of our customers don't notice or care—they just enjoy what we make.

While I know we can never reach every single person with every single allergy or dietary preference, it will always be my goal at Goldenrod Pastries to make our food as inclusive as it can be.

I want you to have a seat at our table!

WOMAN-POWERED BAKING

Like many chefs I know, I learned to bake from my mother and both of my grandmothers. We spent days and days in the kitchen together: preparing for Sunday family dinners, making rolls for holiday meals, birthday cakes, and holiday cookie boxes. We always had our most incredible and substantive conversations while standing over kitchen counters rolling dough and watching sugar boil. Without knowing it, we were solving problems, answering questions and, for me, it was a great way to ask my grandmothers about their lives. My maternal grandmother lived through the Great Depression and my paternal grandmother survived World War II. These two women were my very best friends, and the stories and lives that they lived made me crave more information. I knew that our time in the kitchen was the perfect time to talk.

I work with a predominantly female staff at Goldenrod Pastries. Working well with other women and supporting them to feel empowered, while also feeling that support reciprocated has been one of the most satisfying experiences of my life. They make me feel safe, confident, and unstoppable. And that is what we all need to experience.

My message to women reading this is to find other women who make you feel wonderful. Surround yourself with them, and be one of those women yourself. Find women who want to celebrate you in your moments of greatness and will support you no matter the outcome. Great things happen when women come together. Great things are created.

HOW TO USE THIS BOOK

Along with the recipes, I'm giving you an inside look at the tricks, tips, shortcuts, and nonnegotiables I've learned from almost 20 years in professional kitchens. Diving into this book as a baking newbie? It will be useful for you to read through the supplies, ingredients, and tips sections before you start baking. My goal for you as you work your way through this book, aside from making some really delicious treats, is to learn a little about the processes laid out for you in the recipes. For example, your yeast dough should feel *impossibly fluffy* before it goes in the oven, your cookie dough should be soft but not sticky, your cakes are done when the edges just start to come away from the side of the pan and the cake tops are bouncy to the touch. These are the tricks that hopefully will become intuitive to you as you notice what you're looking for, and how to spot them.

You should also know that at Goldenrod Pastries, we use cup measures to make our treats. I have included weights throughout the book as well, but since we use multiple brands of gluten-free flour, be aware that there is variation in weight between them. We've tried to be a precise as possible, and my recipes are pretty forgiving of a few grams more or less, but double-check the flour bag if you are in doubt.

Perfectly Golden welcomes you into a world where you can learn to bake from what you love to eat and use recipes as a guide along the way.

Welcome to the world of Goldenrod Pastries.

SUPPLIES

These are the baking supplies that I use most often and the supplies that will help you the most when you're baking at home. While this list doesn't include every single pan size referenced in this book, it mentions some basics that will set you up for baking success.

Notice that the items pictured here are not the highest-end or most beautiful supplies. You don't need to invest in top-of-the-line equipment to bake wonderful treats. Start small and start modest. The following is what I use at the bakery every single day—many of these have been with me for over a decade.

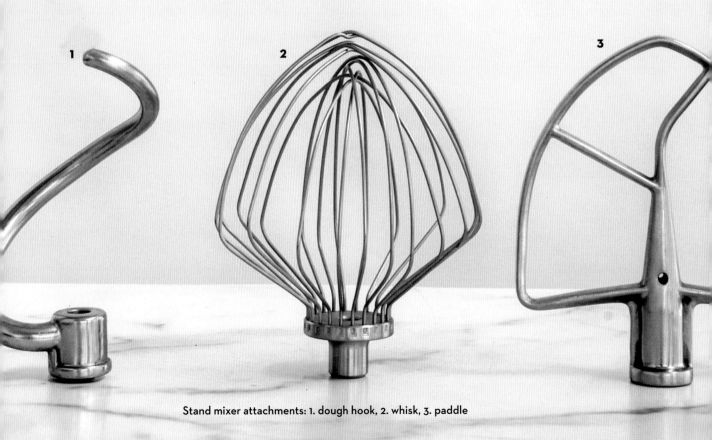

Stand mixer attachments: 1. dough hook, 2. whisk, 3. paddle

1. Mixing bowls

2. Whisks

3. Parchment paper sheets and wax paper rounds

4. Stand mixer

5. Cookie scoops (we use the #30 [2 tablespoons], #24 [2¾ tablespoons], or #20 [3¼ tablespoons] scoops, all by Vollrath)

1. 13-by-18-inch baking sheets

2. Fluted tart pan

3. Baked donut pans and loaf pans

4. Round aluminum cake pans

5. Spatula, rolling pin, wooden spoons

6. Cookie cutters, 1 round pastry tip, and 1 star pastry tip

7. Chef's knife, serrated knife, offset spatula, lifter, small offset spatula, paring knife

8. Cake turntable

9. Containers for organization

10. Heavy-bottomed saucepans

11. Peeler, pastry brush, zester, bench scraper

12. 21-inch pastry piping bags

13. Heatproof rubber spatula

14. Measuring cups and measuring spoons

INGREDIENTS   I started my dairy-free baking journey out of desperation when I couldn't find any treats to eat and didn't know how to make them for myself. After baking for the better part of 25 years, I was suddenly unable to have something that I didn't even consider a luxury in my life, because making and eating pastries had always been my inspiration, my art, and my greatest pleasure. Out of that desperation grew a passion to bake for anyone who wanted a treat— no matter how they chose to eat.

At first, baking dairy-free seemed impossible. But once I got started, I realized that the swaps were pretty straightforward. I started using almond milk in recipes that called for milk, and full-fat canned coconut milk in recipes that called for heavy cream.

Learning the world of gluten-free baking was a steeper learning curve. I tried making dozens of flour blends from well-known bloggers, chefs, and authors. They all tasted fine, but nothing blew me away, and everything absolutely tasted like it was missing something or was made incorrectly. And every time I opened my kitchen cupboards, partially and barely used packages of gums, flours, grains, and seeds fell out, usually spilling their contents everywhere. I didn't end up making any of the flour blends more than one or two times before I gave up, feeling totally disappointed.

When I opened Goldenrod Pastries in 2015, I made a commitment to myself and the community that this bakery would be a place for people to get a birthday cake, or just a cookie on a Wednesday, regardless of how they choose to eat. But that commitment meant I had to figure out a gluten-free flour solution. Luckily, with a little research and a *lot* of trial and error, we figured it out. My sister-in-law, Danielle, a pastry chef who started baking with me shortly after the bakery opened, is fearless in the kitchen. She has a "might as well!" mentality—so we talked through a lot of recipes together and tried a lot of things based on her "might as well!" mentality and our combined 30 years of pastry experience.

Through years of trial and error, I found some excellent gluten-free flours that are commercially available. This means they've already been fully tested in my recipes and are served on a regular basis at Goldenrod Pastries, and they are already mixed and ready for you to start using. And this means you won't have partially used packages of xanthan gum falling on your head when you open a cupboard.

I want to empower you with the knowledge of specific products you can use to make really great and delicious treats based on what we've used for years, to make tens of thousands of pastries.

MILKS

We use only nondairy milks in the bakery, but if you are able to tolerate dairy milk, you can always use it as a one-for-one substitution in any recipe in this book. Here are my favorite nondairy milks to use:

ALMOND MILK This is what we use most of the time. The viscosity of almond milk has nice fattiness, but is still a good liquid consistency. You'll notice that these pour almost like a 1% to 2% standard dairy milk. This is great for buns, cakes, and buttercreams.

OAT MILK, RICE MILK, COCONUT MILK These milks are great alternatives to nut milks. They are a little thinner than nut milks, but they still work well for buns, cakes, and buttercreams.

FULL-FAT CANNED COCONUT MILK Coconut milk is a rich, delicious, and versatile option. Coconut milk has great temperature-fluctuating properties. If it is at room temperature, make sure to shake the can well to distribute the coconut fat and coconut water. When you pour out the coconut milk, it has a really thick consistency, like heavy whipping cream. Once heated, coconut milk becomes thinner, a lot like how butter melts. And when canned coconut milk is cold, the coconut water separates from the fat. This is perfect for Whipped Coconut Cream (page 230).

DAIRY MILK If you prefer to use dairy milk, I recommend 1% or 2% standard dairy milk for these recipes.

EGGS

Eggs can be one of the more challenging ingredients to replace or remove from a recipe. Some recipes in this book can be made with a flax egg replacement; other recipes don't use eggs at all; and there are a few recipes that rely on the stability provided by real eggs for which we do not provide an alternative. A flax egg is a simple mixture of ground flax meal and hot water that, when allowed to sit for a few minutes, offers the same gelling capabilities of eggs. Flax eggs aren't an option for every recipe, but I do denote which recipes allow for that swap. Use the recipe provided here for the recipes that can use flax eggs.

FLAX EGG

This recipe is for one flax egg, so just multiply the ingredients as required for each recipe.

YIELD
1 flax egg

INGREDIENTS
1 tablespoon
   ground flax meal

3 tablespoons hot water

Place the ground flax in a cup or bowl. Add the hot water and stir with a fork until well mixed. Let sit for about 3 minutes, or until the flax has absorbed the water and the mixture has become slightly gelatinous. Use as directed in the recipe.

FATS

COCONUT OIL Coconut oil is very temperature-sensitive. We use it only in its melted state. Coconut oil is great for the B.A.B.E. Square crust (page 186), the crumble from The Original Crumble-Bun (page 64) for buns and muffins, and it is awesome in Goldenrod's Favorite Lemon Curd (page 236). I also use it in my Funeral Brownies (page 124). I like to use melted coconut oil when I would normally use melted butter. I typically use refined coconut oil when baking, as it has a higher smoke point.

VEGETABLE SHORTENING I tried so hard to find a great dairy-free butter alternative that didn't leave off-flavors in my pastries, but I never found anything that works as well as vegetable shortening. I prefer Crisco brand over anything generic, but you can also try an organic, nonhydrogenated brand. I've had good luck with those as well. This is a great ingredient for our Base Cookie recipe (page 76) and Classic Vanilla Buttercream (page 223). If you need to bake vegan or dairy-free, avoid vegetable shortening labeled "butter flavor," as the "natural flavors" in the ingredients may derive from dairy. If you need to avoid soy, look for a shortening that uses other fats, such as coconut or palm oil.

BUTTER Butter can add a nice taste to recipes, so if you are comfortable eating dairy, feel free to use it! Unsalted butter or vegetable shortening can be used one for one in the recipes in this book.

OLIVE OIL Olive oil is a great ingredient for some cakes in this book. I do call for vegetable oil in some of our cakes, but you are welcome to use olive oil if you prefer the flavor.

NEUTRAL OIL Vegetable oil is a great, basic oil. It is derived from soy, but the soy protein is removed in processing, so this may be a safe option for people with soy protein allergies. As in all cases with allergens, however, please check the label and consult with your doctor, if necessary. You can also use sunflower oil, safflower oil, or grapeseed oil—all soy-free—if you prefer. These are all great neutral oils for the recipes in this book.

NONSTICK SPRAY Some recipes call for spraying a pan with nonstick spray. If you need to bake vegan or dairy-free, avoid nonstick sprays labeled "butter flavor," as the "natural flavors" in the ingredients may derive from dairy. If you need to bake gluten-free, be sure to select a nonstick spray that is completely flour-free.

GLUTEN-FREE FLOURS AND SALT

One of the coolest and most rewarding parts of baking with the following gluten-free flours is that they actually make some recipes *even better* than they are with traditional all-purpose flour. These flours use delicious ingredients, such as sorghum flour that adds a nutty flavor and a really soft texture. When we usually have to be concerned with overmixing a cake batter or cookie dough when using all-purpose flour, that isn't a concern with most of these flours. Just check the notes for each recipe to understand how each works best for each application.

If you are baking the gluten-free versions of the recipes in this book, I recommend using the flour that I suggest for each recipe (see the **Angela Says** notes in the recipes). If you are gluten tolerant, you can use standard all-purpose flour.

If you are unable to find these specific flours, you can find an alternative flour that has a similar ingredient list. Notice *the order* of the ingredients—they are listed in order of percentage used.

SUPPLIES

BOB'S RED MILL GLUTEN FREE 1 TO 1 BAKING FLOUR This brand makes two different gluten-free baking flours. The one that I recommend here is made predominantly with sweet and brown rice flours—**be sure to use the 1 to 1 version of Bob's Red Mill Baking Flour.** The other version is made primarily with garbanzo bean flour and a higher ratio of gums, which makes a thicker, stickier batter. I use this flour in the Best Pound Cake recipe (page 131), and other snack cakes, such as our Base Muffin recipe (page 148).

MAIN INGREDIENTS: Sweet rice flour, brown rice flour, potato starch, sorghum flour, xanthan gum

Angela Says

✳ I've spent the past six years finding the best ingredients for the recipes in this book. I wanted to find a way to make my favorite recipes dairy-free to fit my needs, and gluten-free (and beyond) to meet the needs of my friends and customers. The flours I recommend will make your treats exactly like the ones I make at Goldenrod Pastries, but if you can't easily find them, do your best to buy something close to it. Check your local grocery stores and co-ops first, then go on-line. Your final product might differ slightly, but you will still make something delicious!

NU LIFE ALWAYS GLUTEN FREE ALL-PURPOSE FLOUR This is one of my very favorite flours. It is sorghum-based flour that has just a little bit of potato starch, tapioca starch, and xanthan gum. This flour makes the most delicious cookies, such as my favorite Double Chocolate Cookies (page 80). This is the one flour blend I've tried that makes the classic soft-center cookie with a slightly crisp outside edge. Sorghum makes a very soft flour, one that lends itself primarily to cookies, but also some cakes. You do need to order this flour directly from the company's website. They have excellent customer service, shipping is fast, and the product is outstanding.

MAIN INGREDIENTS: Sorghum flour, potato starch, xanthan gum

PAMELA'S GLUTEN-FREE ALL-PURPOSE BAKING FLOUR This is the most challenging flour that we use at Goldenrod. It uses more gums to stabilize the flour, which works great in the Extra Special Banana Bread (page 132). This flour tastes very light in layer cakes, such as the Champagne Cake with Almond Buttercream (page 206). When you use this flour, be sure to keep an eye on the batter. It is easy to overmix (the only flour I recommend that is easy to overmix), but it makes a really wonderful product once you get the hang of it. If it seems as if you over-mixed a cake batter using this flour, add an additional ¼ to ½ cup (63 to 125 ml) of your choice of milk and fold it in gently. This fixes it every time.

MAIN INGREDIENTS: Brown rice flour, tapioca starch, white rice flour, potato starch, sorghum flour, guar gum (this is the most important ingredient for the recipes where this flour is used)

ALMOND FLOUR Almond flour is a very fatty flour that creates a shortbread-like consistency and is great to use in tart crusts, such as in the Chocolate Ganache Tart (page 152). It's also awesome in rich cakes, such as the Lemon + Almond Torte (page 110). I don't like to use almond flour in too many cakes, though, because it can create a really dense texture. It is delicious used in such cookies as the Chewy Almond Cookies (page 95). If you are allergic to almonds, please do not substitute other flours—choose another, safe recipe in the book.

KING ARTHUR FLOUR GLUTEN FREE MEASURE FOR MEASURE FLOUR This is a very fine flour and is the closest to a traditional cake flour of the gluten-free flours listed here—I love how fluffy and light it is. This flour produces very airy and cakey results, which I like for heavier and less sweet recipes, such as the Gingerbread Cookie Cutouts (page 104) and Funeral Brownies (page 124). Like Bob's Red Mill, King Arthur makes multiple gluten-free flours. **Make sure you are using the Measure for Measure flour,** not the all-purpose gluten-free flour.

MAIN INGREDIENTS: Rice flour, whole grain rice flour, sorghum flour, tapioca starch, potato starch, xantham gum

USE SALT IN EVERY BAKED GOOD That's it, that's the tip. With just a small addition of sea salt, your tarts will taste sweeter, your fruit will taste brighter, and your chocolate will taste more like chocolate. All of these recipes were developed using fine sea salt. If you use coarse kosher salt, use a touch more than you would with fine sea salt or table salt.

BASIC INGREDIENTS TO KEEP IN YOUR PANTRY

If you want to be prepared to bake on a whim, keep these basic ingredients in your pantry.

- Granulated sugar, brown sugar, baking powder, baking soda, fine sea salt, warm spices such as cinnamon, flour(s), unsalted butter or vegetable shortening, a container of shelf-stable almond or your preferred non-dairy milk, canned coconut milk, and pure vanilla extract.

- If you are baking the gluten-free recipe versions in this book, be sure to keep your favorite gluten-free flour on hand. If you think you'll make a lot of cookies, buy Nu Life Always Gluten Free All-Purpose Flour or the King Arthur Gluten Free Measure for Measure Flour. If you are more of a layer cake or bun person, keep Pamela's Gluten-Free All-Purpose Flour on hand. And, if you're more apt to make snack cakes and brownies, get Bob's Red Mill Gluten Free 1 to 1 Baking Flour. If you need to bake gluten-free, check that your baking powder is labeled gluten-free.

BAKING TIPS

I wish I could be in your kitchen with you. I wish we could bake a batch of cookies together, and shape and glaze buns together. We could talk about the best place in your kitchen to let dough rise, and watch a cake bake through the oven door. And take a skinny slice of the very end of a pound cake loaf when it's still too hot to cut properly.

This section will be the next best thing to us baking together in your kitchen. It's important to remember that these recipes and the instructions are guidelines that work for me and for the other people who have baked these recipes—*but* all our kitchens, ovens, climates, and altitudes are different. My goal at Goldenrod is to always arm my bakers with the knowledge of how something is supposed to look and feel, instead of following rigid guidelines. If I can help you understand what you should see and feel for a cake to be done, or a cinnamon roll that is ready to be baked, you will be baking successfully through this book and long after.

There's a story about this: At one point, I brought on two bakers at the same time at Goldenrod. They saw that our recipes simply read "salt," or "vanilla," or even "spices," with no measurements listed. They asked where to find working oven timers, as the one built into our convection oven had recently stopped working. I told them, "You'll know when it's done," which at first they didn't believe and looked at me, stunned. When they asked what quantity of salt to use for recipes without an amount specified, I would walk over to look in their bowl at what they were making, curl up my hand, and draw a circle in it with the other hand, and say "About that much." It only took about one month before they started answering those questions on their own.

In this cookbook, I will provide cooking times, temperatures, and measurements. I do want you to grow confident in your own instincts. Perfectly Golden, to me, means a cake or cookies or buns that you pull from the oven will be golden from the heat and perfect because you made it.

Baking and being in the kitchen gives me a sense of freedom that I feel very

few other places. In fact, I think the basis for feeling free anywhere, for me, always stems from the kitchen. Start with recipes in this book that you feel are familiar to you. Become comfortable with those, then allow yourself to branch out.

All the recipes in this book are tested and accurate. The tips in this section will help account for differences in our environments, and help you reach a place of freedom and pleasure in your own kitchen.

TIPS FOR YEAST DOUGH

WHY DOUGH DOESN'T RISE There are generally two reasons yeast-leavened dough doesn't rise. Either the milk added at the beginning of the recipe was too hot and killed the yeast, or the yeast you're using was already dead. To prevent killing the yeast, heat your milk to only 105° to 110°F. And if you have yeast that you don't think you'll use within a month, store it in the freezer until you're ready to use it.

HOW TO HELP DOUGH RISE Dough rises in warm environments, so try to keep it warm the entire time you are working with it. This speeds up the process, and also ensures that your yeast stays active the entire time. When you are letting your dough rise for the first time, try this tip: fill your kitchen sink with about 5 inches of warm water. Place the bowl of dough in the water, and gently cover the dough with a clean tea towel. This is a tip from my grandma Garbacz.

HOW TO KNOW YOUR BUNS ARE READY TO BAKE The time guidelines in my recipes are the times that have worked well for me when I follow all of these tips. If your buns don't seem to have risen very much during that time period, give them some more time. When you gently poke a perfectly risen bun, it should give back to your touch and slowly return to its original shape.

TIPS FOR CAKES

WHAT TO DO WITH THICK CAKE BATTER If you are using the gluten-free recipe versions in this book, there is a chance your batter could get overmixed and a little too thick. A perfectly mixed cake batter will flow easily out of your mixing bowl. If your batter seems thick and hard to pour, add an additional ¼ to ½ cup of dairy or nondairy milk and gently fold it in until it is just barely combined.

HOW TO KNOW WHEN CAKE IS FULLY BAKED There are approximate bake times for every recipe in this book. Because all of our kitchen environments vary, your baking time might also vary. The edges of a fully baked cake will start to come away from the sides of the pan. Also, when you gently poke the center of the cake, the cake should not have any give and will bounce back immediately. You can also insert a paring knife or toothpick into the center of the cake to check for doneness. If it comes out clean, the cake is baked.

REMOVING CAKES FROM PANS Run a butter knife around the edge of the pan, between the cake and the pan. Make sure the knife stays in contact with the side of the pan the entire time—this ensures you will have a nice edge on the cake and you aren't cutting into the cake itself.

COOLING CAKES I like to let layer cakes cool in their pans. This lets the outside of the cake almost steam a little, keeping the edges really soft. For such cakes as banana bread or pound cake, I like to unmold them from their pans after about 10 minutes. These cakes do well cooling outside their pans so they form a bit more of a crust. You can take them out of their pans and let them cool directly on the plate you'll use for serving, or on a piece of parchment paper. I don't believe a cooling rack is necessary.

DECORATING CAKES If you are working a day in advance, and have a little extra time, I recommend this hack: decorate cake layers when they are frozen. Once

they have cooled and you have used a serrated knife to even the top of each layer, freeze them in a single layer (each wrapped in plastic wrap), and then stack them to decorate. An offset spatula is the easiest decorating tool here. Or you can fill, stack, and decorate the cakes when the layers are completely cool.

TIPS FOR COOKIES

MAKING COOKIE DOUGH The cookie dough in this book should always have about the same consistency—fluffy, but not too sticky. It should not stick to your hands or other utensils too much. If your cookie dough seems a little too sticky, add more flour, starting with ¼ cup at a time.

SCOOPING COOKIES We use a #24 scoop (about 2¾ tablespoons) at the bakery to shape cookies. You are welcome to use two soup spoons to drop the cookies onto baking sheets if you don't want to buy a special scoop—but I do think you'll really like using the scoop!

FREEZING COOKIE DOUGH If you don't want to make your cookies right away, you can freeze them as individual scoops. I recommend scooping and forming the cookies, then freezing them until you are ready to use them, as opposed to refrigerating a bowl full of cookie dough. Then, you can take out the unbaked cookies and put them straight into the oven. Baking frozen cookies adds 3 to 4 minutes to your total baking time.

BAKING COOKIES Here are a few different cookie-baking techniques: You can press down each cookie with the bottom of a glass or the palm of your hand before they go into the oven. Or you can try the Goldenrod cookie method: we put the pan of cookie dough balls directly into the oven, then use a piece of parchment paper or wax paper to press down each cookie at 5 to 7 minutes into the baking time. Both techniques give a good cookie height and make sure they don't end up too domed on top. If you prefer a domed cookie, don't smash them! Remove cookies from the oven when their edges are perfectly golden brown and don't give back when you gently press them. The center of each cookie should be slightly risen and have a matte finish. Shiny cookie centers mean that they are not fully baked.

COOLING COOKIES I recommend letting your cookies cool directly on the baking sheet—when you pull your cookies out of the oven at the right time, when the edges are perfectly golden and the centers just have a matte finish, they can stand to stay on the hot baking sheet until they are cool. If you take your cookies out of the oven and they look a little darker than "perfectly golden," remove them from the baking sheet with a metal spatula and transfer them to either a plate or a cooling rack. The hot baking sheet continues to heat and bake the cookies, so if they are a little more done, they will end up being overbaked—but when you take them out of the oven just as I recommend, they'll be just great with the extra few minutes of residual heat from the hot baking sheet.

STORING TREATS

Cakes, buns, and cookies are best stored either at room temperature or frozen. Refrigeration will degrade the starch in your products pretty quickly and you'll be left with stale pastries. If you are going to eat something within a day or two, I always recommend leaving it at room temperature. The freezer is best if you are going to keep the treats longer or want to save them for a future event or a rainy day.

My pro tip for long-term storage is to freeze any leftover cake in slices individually plastic-wrapped or in airtight containers. That way, you can pull out a piece at a time and either eat it cold or let it defrost faster than waiting for a whole cake. I learned this from experience and can highly recommend planning ahead for yourself and keeping slices of cake in your freezer. Because you will want it. And you won't want to wait.

There are some hard-and-fast rules you really can't change, and we will go over those—but otherwise, I want you to be your own chef. Learn how to make it work from what you have on hand. Build your pantry so that you are always just an hour away from a homemade cake.

HOW TO USE THE "YOU DO YOU" KEY

As different readers may have different dietary needs, the "You Do You" key at the top of each recipe allows you to see at a glance whether your needs can be met by choosing the appropriate alternative among the ingredients. If there is no listing for your particular dietary requirement, it means this recipe should not be made with any alternative ingredients—but there are plenty of other delicious recipes in this book that will meet your needs. The key may contain any of these options:

GLUTEN-FREE Can be made totally free of gluten

DAIRY-FREE Can be made totally free of dairy products (milk, cream, butter, etc.)

VEGAN Can be made totally free of animal products (dairy, eggs, honey, gelatin)

TRADITIONAL Can be made with traditional baking ingredients that may include gluten, dairy, and other animal products

Please review the ingredients lists carefully if you need to accommodate an allergy or sensitivity not listed in the "You Do You" key.

BUNS + YEASTED TREATS

Yeasted dough was my first real love in the kitchen, the first thing I really latched on to. I learned how to make dough from my Polish grandma, who I called Baba. Aside from being one of my very best friends, she was a very good, and very deliberate, cook.

I was allowed to make rolls for holidays with my grandma and was honored when she decided to teach me how to make her infamous Peach Coffee Cake (page 71). In my kitchen now, I try to play around with how my doughs rise and at which temperature I'll bake them. By doing so, I change and (hopefully) improve the final product. I love how personal and tangible that process is.

Anyone who knows me, knows that if I have a chance to touch or poke any food, especially pastries, I'll take it. *How much will a dough squish? How soft is that cake's crumb?* My friends just know that if they have cake or a bun in front of them, I'm probably going to ask to touch it.

It's sensory for me. With buns, I feel the temperature of the milk; smell the yeast as it blooms; hear the salt, oil, and flour fall into the bowl; watch the dough as it starts to mix and then completely change. Then, I poke the dough to make sure it's the correct consistency. I smell it and watch it as it grows in its warm environment. I see and hear the proofed dough fall out of the bowl onto a floured surface, with a cloud of flour going *poof* into the air. I roll it out. It's so sensual and tangible. My hands in the dough; the satisfying sound of a sharp knife cutting each bun; poking a few buns before they go in the oven, to make sure they have risen *just enough*. Smelling them bake. Glazing them at the perfect temperature and with the perfect glaze consistency. It's all pleasure to me.

Learning to make buns is the last step in our baker training process at Goldenrod. It is so intimate and personal to each person. It's a beautiful thing to watch our bakers develop their own personal method and grow in their bun making.

There is a mad dash to our bun section at Goldenrod every morning. People are so excited to see the daily selection. They see The Original Crumble-Bun (page 64) flavor, choose the bun that speaks to them, then move on to get situated with their coffee and buns. It's a culture. It's a feeling.

RICH BUN DOUGH

This is the epitome of a super fluffy, light bun dough and what we use for our gluten-free buns. We tried so many different versions before settling on what's in this recipe. I'm very passionate about buns and always want to make sure every version is as satisfying and wonderful as the original version. I never want to make something that is simply "good for being gluten-free" and always strive to develop recipes that are delicious, no matter what is or isn't in them.

This dough comes together very differently than Goldenrod's Favorite Egg-Free Bun Dough (page 51). It does use eggs, which helps the dough hold together and adds some additional richness. When you're working through bun recipes in this chapter, make sure you follow the method and the tips and tricks in this recipe for the best outcome.

YOU DO YOU
MAKE THIS
- ☐ vegan
- ✗ dairy-free
- ✗ gluten-free
- ✗ traditional

YIELD
12 buns

INGREDIENTS

1½ cups (360 ml) milk, almond milk or your favorite nondairy milk

¾ cup (150 g) granulated sugar

2 tablespoons active dry yeast

⅓ cup (80 ml) vegetable oil

2 large eggs

1 teaspoon sea salt

4¼ cups (531 g) all-purpose flour or 4¼ cups gluten-free all-purpose flour, plus appropriate flour for dusting

Angela Says

✳ For the gluten-free flour, I recommend Pamela's Gluten-Free All-Purpose Flour (510 g).

✳ Your yeast mixture is bloomed and ready when it has a beautiful, fluffy, frothy mass on top, a slight yeast aroma, and the top frothy layer moves as one unit when you wiggle the bowl a little.

Bloom the yeast: Heat your milk to about 110°F. Any hotter and you will kill your yeast; much cooler and your yeast will take a very long time to activate. It should be warm to the touch. Pour the warm milk into the bowl of a stand mixer and add your sugar and yeast. Use a handheld whisk to combine. I like to set the bowl on top of a preheating oven to bloom, but your counter is fine, too. This takes about 10 minutes.

Mix the dough: Once the yeast has bloomed, add the oil, eggs, and salt. Using a stand mixer fitted with a paddle attachment for gluten-free flour, mix on low speed to break up the eggs and to combine all the ingredients. If you're using traditional flour, switch to the dough hook attachment. Add the flour and mix on low speed until all the ingredients are combined and the dough has come together into a cohesive ball, 1 to 2 minutes.

Gluten-free dough rises fairly quickly and is very tender, so you don't need to knead it or let it rise between mixing the dough and rolling out and shaping the final product. For traditional flour, you'll need to let the dough rise—there are many different approaches to this. I like to set the bowl of dough on top of a preheating oven. This works well and moves the process along pretty quickly. If you need to speed up the rise time, put a clean towel or some plastic wrap over the bowl to keep the dough warmer. You can also fill your sink with about 5 inches of warm water, cover the dough with a clean tea towel, and set the bowl in the water. Your dough is ready to use when it looks as if it has doubled in size. When you press the dough a little, it should feel supple, soft, and have some more give. Yeast stays busy and dough rises when it is warm, so do your best to keep a warm environment for the dough as it rises.

At this point, you are ready to make buns of your choosing. Experiment with the recipes in this chapter, then try your hand at making your own bun dough recipe based on what you love.

When you are ready to make buns using the gluten-free version of this dough, remember to roll out the dough on a very well-floured piece of parchment paper or silicone mat. This prevents the dough from losing its structure and will help you to roll out the dough to the correct size. Use the parchment paper or mat to roll up the dough. Simply lift the paper with both hands and use it to roll the dough forward, instead of using your hands. Keep going until it's fully rolled.

EGG-FREE BUN DOUGH

We spent years creating and refining a streamlined base recipe for vegan buns—it is customizable for many different recipes, impossibly fluffy, and with the proper method, will teach you so much about yeast dough and how it acts.

This recipe uses all-purpose flour. Try Goldenrod's Favorite Rich Bun Dough (page 48) if you need a gluten-free bun recipe.

(page 48)

YOU DO YOU

MAKE THIS

✗ vegan
✗ dairy-free
☐ gluten-free
✗ traditional

YIELD

12 buns

INGREDIENTS

1½ cups (360 ml) milk, almond milk, or your favorite nondairy milk

½ cup (100 g) granulated sugar

2 tablespoons active dry yeast

⅓ cup (80 ml) vegetable oil

1 teaspoon sea salt

5 cups (625 g) all-purpose flour, plus more for dusting

Angela Says

✳ Try this recipe a few times to find what you love about it. Working with yeast dough is a very personal experience, and sometimes takes a couple of times to feel like you've really found your way!

✳ Keep your dough warm throughout the entire process—from the time you add the sugar and yeast to the milk through to the rising, etc. Keep it warm and the process will move quickly and will be most successful.

✳ Your yeast mixture is bloomed and ready when it has a beautiful, fluffy, frothy mass on top, a slight yeast aroma, and the top frothy layer moves as one unit when you wiggle the bowl a little.

Bloom the yeast: Heat your milk to about 110°F. Any hotter and you will kill your yeast; much cooler and your yeast will take a very long time to activate. It should be warm to the touch. Pour the warm milk into the bowl of a stand mixer (or a large bowl) and add your sugar and yeast. Use a handheld whisk to combine. I like to set the bowl on top of a preheating oven to bloom, but your counter is fine, too. This takes about 10 minutes.

Mix the dough: Once the yeast has bloomed, add the oil, salt, and flour to your yeast mixture. Using a stand mixer fitted with a hook attachment, mix on medium-low speed until a smooth ball of dough is formed, 8 to 10 minutes.

Alternatively, use a wooden spoon to mix all your ingredients into as much of a cohesive mass as possible. From there, you can either turn it out onto a lightly floured counter and knead by hand for 10 minutes or try the method I was taught: use your fists to punch down the dough over and over. My grandma folded the dough over every few punches.

Let the dough rise: There are a lot of different approaches to this. I like to set the bowl of dough on top of a preheating oven. This works well and moves the process along pretty quickly. If you need to speed up the rise time, put a clean towel or some plastic wrap over the bowl to keep the dough warmer. You can also fill your sink with about 5 inches of warm water, cover the dough with a clean tea towel, and set the bowl in the water. Your dough is ready to use when it looks as if it has doubled in size. When you press the dough a little, it should feel supple, soft, and have some more give. Yeast stays busy and dough rises when it is warm, so do your best to keep a warm environment for the dough as it rises.

At this point, you are ready to make buns of your choosing. Experiment with the recipes in this chapter, then try your hand at making your own bun recipe based off what you love.

CINNAMON ROLLS

YOU
DO **YOU**

MAKE THIS
✗ vegan
✗ dairy-free
✗ gluten-free
✗ traditional

This is one of the most exciting recipes in the book. This is a recipe that I hope you make once and realize that it's really something you can whip up fast to have ready to share at brunches, to take to parties, and even to make for yourself on a slow weekend morning. It's a recipe that I hope gets dog-eared in this book and that you go back to for many years to come.

Whether you use Goldenrod's Favorite Rich Bun Dough or Goldenrod's Favorite Egg-Free Bun Dough for this recipe, I'm sure you'll be so thrilled with the results.

YIELD

12 buns

INGREDIENTS

1 recipe Goldenrod's Favorite Bun Dough of your choice (page 48 or page 51), plus appropriate flour for dusting

5⅓ tablespoons (75 g) unsalted butter or ⅓ cup (64 g) vegetable shortening

1 cup (179 g) light brown sugar

¼ cup (25 g) ground cinnamon

1 recipe Classic Vanilla Glaze (page 221)

Preheat your oven to 375°F and line two baking sheets with parchment paper.

Roll out your choice of dough to a 10-by-20-inch rectangle, keeping the rolling surface lightly floured and moving the dough a little after each roll. You don't want it to stick, and the best way to make sure it isn't sticking is to keep checking. Use more flour as needed.

If you are using the egg-free bun dough, spread your choice of fat over the surface of the dough with a rubber spatula. If you are using the gluten-free bun dough, melt your choice of fat first and brush it on the surface of the dough with a pastry brush. Evenly spread the brown sugar across the surface of the dough, making sure to get it to every edge and corner. Then, sprinkle with the cinnamon, again making sure it reaches every edge and corner. Roll up the dough, starting from a long end and moving up. Make sure it is a tight swirl. Using a sharp chef's knife and working down the length of the roll, cut into 12 1½-inch wheels.

Arrange the buns in the prepared pans, about 2 inches apart. We always tuck the tails at Goldenrod. The "tail" is the end of each bun—grab it and fold it under the roll. This gives each person a really special bit at the bottom of each bun. See the photos on pages 54–57 for a demonstration of this technique.

Let rise in a warm place until the dough is very fluffy to the touch and your finger leaves a slight indentation when you gently poke the edge, about 25 minutes. Bake for 35 minutes, until the buns are perfectly golden brown all over and the centers of each roll do not give back at all when you press them lightly.

Remove from the oven and glaze immediately with Classic Vanilla Glaze, which we dollop on using a #20 scoop, about 3¼ tablespoons (see page 23). Enjoy warm, or within the next 12 to 24 hours.

Angela Says

✱ Roll out gluten-free dough on a very well-floured piece of parchment paper or silicone mat. This prevents the dough from losing its structure and will help you to roll out the dough to the correct size. If the dough feels fragile after the filling has been spread, use the parchment paper or mat to roll up the dough. Simply lift the paper with both hands and use it to roll the dough forward, instead of using your hands. Keep going until it's fully rolled.

STICKY PECAN BUNS

The best thing that happened when we started making these buns in the shop was having my dad try the first batch. Between him and my grandmother who taught me how to make yeast dough, I found my true love for buns. He's my measure of what is a good bun—the man who has to have one sip of coffee for every bite of pastry. The man who would go around town before we woke up, going to three different pastry shops, just to make sure he brought home everyone's favorite bun or donut. Goldenrod had extra caramel on a Saturday morning, so I tried a pan of sticky buns, full of pecans. He tried the first one, and was so excited about how light they were. I told him that maybe the vegan caramel made it less rich than sticky buns he had traditionally eaten. "Yeah, maybe it's because they are vegan," he said.

The edges of these buns are my favorite part. The way the caramel bakes into the dough and clings to the sides of the pan is so deluxe. The centers are so flaky and you get just a drip of caramel in each bite. And the pecans that stick to the inside of the pan? You're lucky if you can nab those for yourself.

YIELD

12 buns

INGREDIENTS

1 recipe Goldenrod's Favorite Bun Dough of your choice (page 48 or page 51), plus appropriate flour for dusting

Nonstick spray for pan

1 cup (240 ml) Caramel Sauce (page 234)

3 cups (537 g) light brown sugar

3 cups (375 g) pecan pieces

5⅓ tablespoons (75 g) unsalted butter or ⅓ cup (64 g) vegetable shortening

¼ cup (25 g) ground cinnamon

Angela Says

✱ Roll out gluten-free dough on a very well-floured piece of parchment paper or silicone mat. This prevents the dough from losing its structure and will help you to roll out the dough to the correct size. If the dough feels fragile after the filling has been spread, use the parchment paper or mat to roll up the dough. Simply lift the paper with both hands and use it to roll the dough forward, instead of using your hands. Keep going until it's fully rolled.

Preheat your oven to 400°F. Spray a 9-by-13-inch baking pan liberally with nonstick spray. Pour the caramel sauce into the bottom of the pan, spreading it evenly, followed by sprinkling 1 cup (179 g) of the brown sugar over the caramel. Cover the caramel and brown sugar with the pecan pieces. Set aside.

Roll out your choice of dough into a 12-by-20-inch rectangle, keeping the rolling surface lightly floured and moving the dough a little after each roll. You don't want it to stick, and the best way to make sure it isn't sticking is to keep checking. Use more flour as needed.

If you're using the egg-free bun dough, spread your choice of fat over the surface of the dough with a rubber spatula. If you are using the gluten-free bun dough, melt the fat first and brush it on the surface of the dough with a pastry brush. Evenly spread the remaining 2 cups (358 g) of brown sugar across the surface of the dough, making sure to get it to every edge and corner. Then, sprinkle with the cinnamon, again making sure it reaches every edge and corner. Roll up the dough, starting from a long end and moving up. Make sure it is a tight swirl. Using a sharp chef's knife and working down the length of the roll, cut into 12 1½-inch wheels.

Arrange the buns closely in the prepared pan. We always tuck the tails at Goldenrod. The "tail" is the end of each bun—grab it and fold it under the roll. This gives each person a really special bit at the bottom of each bun. See the photos on pages 54–57 for a demonstration of this technique. The buns will touch one another in the pan, and that is perfectly good! They will rise together as they bake.

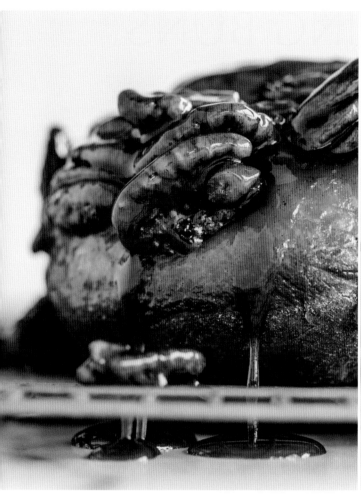

Let rise in a warm place until the dough is very fluffy to the touch and your finger leaves a slight indentation when you gently poke the edge, about 20 minutes.

I recommend putting the pan on top of a baking sheet so that any caramel that bubbles over lands on that second pan, and not on the bottom of your oven. Bake for 35 to 45 minutes, until the buns are perfectly golden brown and the centers of each roll do not give back at all when you press them lightly. This part is key. Because they are baking as a unit in the pan, the baking time can be a little longer.

Remove from the oven and let cool in the pan for 5 to 10 minutes, before *carefully* unmolding onto a separate rimmed baking sheet large enough to collect any excess caramel. *Keep in mind that you are working with a hot sugar syrup, so please use caution so as to not burn yourself!* Enjoy warm, or within the next 12 to 24 hours.

✳ Looks can be deceiving. The color of these buns may be darker than you expect. To make sure these are fully baked, let them bake until the center does not bounce back *at all* when you gently press on it.

✳ Make sure you unmold these from their pan within 5 to 10 minutes of coming out of the oven. Once the caramel cools down in the pan, it is harder to unmold, plus you'll miss that luscious drip of caramel down the sides of your buns.

✳ You can assemble the pan of buns, cover with plastic wrap, and store overnight in the fridge. Pop the uncovered pan into the oven once you turn it on to preheat. The preheat time will give the buns a chance to warm up and rise a little, just in time for the oven to be up to its final temperature.

MORNING BUNS

I first tasted a morning bun on an anniversary trip with my husband to the Bay Area in 2019. It was a simple twist of dough, dusted with aromatic orange sugar. Always looking for new buns to make, I decided this would be a great one to add to our list at Goldenrod. It became an instant classic for both staff and customers. We started with the one I had already tried—a simple bun rolled up, brushed with a citrus syrup, and dusted with orange sugar. One of my bakers, Amber, had extra dough to use one morning and I suggested she make any kind of bun she wanted. She chose a morning bun with lemon sugar and poppy seeds. Talk about a stunner! I try not to choose favorites, but this is one of my top five recipes in this book. I hope you love it as much as we do!

Because the flavor of the dough really shines through in this simple bun, I suggest making your dough a day or two in advance, wrapping it well in plastic wrap, and letting it sit in your refrigerator for at least one day, but two is even better. That time in the refrigerator allows the dough to ferment at a safe temperature, which adds a more pronounced yeast flavor to the dough and finished product. I also recommend making your citrus sugars a day or two early, so the oils from the lemon and orange zest have a chance to perfume the sugar completely.

You're welcome to make these from start to finish in the same day, but for a really exceptional bun experience, plan ahead on this one and start the dough and sugars in advance.

YOU
DO **YOU**

MAKE THIS

X̶ vegan

X̶ dairy-free

X̶ gluten-free

X̶ traditional

YIELD

12 buns

BUNS

1 recipe Goldenrod's Favorite Bun Dough of your choice (page 48 or page 51), plus appropriate flour for dusting

4 tablespoons (½ stick, 55 g) unsalted butter or ¼ cup (48 g) vegetable shortening

1 cup (200 g) granulated sugar

Zest of either 1 orange or 2 lemons

¼ cup (34 g) poppy seeds (optional)

CITRUS SYRUP

1½ cups (300 g) granulated sugar

Juice of 1 orange or 2 lemons

1 cup (240 ml) water

TO FINISH BUNS

2 cups (400 g) granulated sugar

Prepare the buns: Prepare your choice of dough, wrapping it tightly in plastic wrap after its first rise. I recommend wrapping it two times. Allow the dough to rest and ferment in your refrigerator for 24 to 48 hours.

Place the sugar and your choice of citrus zest in a bowl. Use your hands to combine, making sure that the zest is evenly distributed throughout the sugar. Transfer to an airtight container or wrap the bowl with plastic wrap. Keep this citrus sugar at room temperature until you are ready to make your buns.

Remove your dough from the refrigerator and let it come to room temperature for about 1 hour before you begin to roll it out.

Preheat your oven to 350°F and line two baking sheets with a fitted sheet of parchment paper.

Roll out the dough to a 10-by-20-inch rectangle, keeping the rolling surface lightly floured and moving the dough a little after each roll. You don't want it to stick, and the best way to make sure it isn't sticking is to keep checking. Use more flour as needed.

If you are using the egg-free bun dough, spread your choice of fat over the surface of the dough with a rubber spatula. If you are using the gluten-free bun dough, melt your choice of fat first and brush it on the surface of the dough with a pastry brush. Evenly spread the citrus sugar across the surface of the dough, making sure it reaches every edge and corner. If you are using the lemon sugar, sprinkle with the poppy seeds (if

✳ Roll out gluten-free dough on a very well-floured piece of parchment paper or silicone mat. This prevents the dough from losing its structure and will help you to roll out the dough to the correct size. If the dough feels fragile after the filling has been spread, use the parchment paper or mat to roll up the dough. Simply lift the paper with both hands and use it to roll the dough forward, instead of using your hands. Keep going until it's fully rolled.

using), again making sure it reaches every edge and corner. Roll up the dough, starting from a long end and moving up. Make sure it is a tight swirl. Using a sharp chef's knife and working down the length of the roll, cut into 2-inch wheels.

Arrange the buns in the prepared pans, about 2 inches apart. We always tuck the tails at Goldenrod. The "tail" is the end of each bun—grab it and fold it under the roll. This gives each person a really special bit at the bottom of each bun. See the photos on pages 54–57 for a demonstration of this technique.

Let rise in a warm place until the dough is very fluffy to the touch and your finger leaves a slight indentation when you gently poke the edge, about 25 minutes. Bake for 35 minutes, until the buns are perfectly golden brown all over and the centers of each roll do not give back at all when you press them lightly.

Prepare the citrus syrup: Place the sugar and citrus juice in a heavy-bottomed small pot. Add the water, mix well, and allow to come to a boil. Immediately take the syrup off the heat after it reaches the boil.

Finish the buns: Place the granulated sugar in a large bowl. Brush each bun with the citrus syrup, making sure to brush around the sides as well. Place each bun in the bowl of sugar, using your hands or a spoon to cover the top and sides of each bun in sugar, tapping off any excess.

Serve the same day.

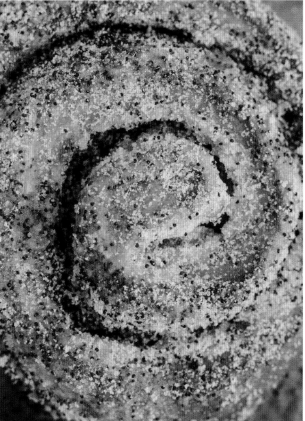

THE ORIGINAL
CRUMBLE-BUN

I started making the original version of these buns in the fall of 2015, about six months after the shop opened. We had so many cranberries and had used most of them for preserves. It was right around Thanksgiving, so we were making cranberry everything: scones, layered cakes, muffins, etc. I think it was a Saturday morning when I decided to make a bun with some of the remaining cranberry preserves. Looking back on it, the first version was pretty pathetic. I stretched a blob of sweet roll dough into a long cylinder, sliced off chunks, and pushed cranberry preserves into the center. It really was delicious, but there was too much dough and not enough other stuff. I thought about adding some crunchy texture on the top, and the idea of using crumble came to mind. I kept using the same method and started adding some crumble on each bun—but it still wasn't right.

Eventually I realized that the dough needed to be swirled with sugar throughout the bun. I swirled it with some fat as well, like a cinnamon roll but without the cinnamon. I can't recall how long this process lasted, but I do remember sharing the first successful, most wonderful version with Lesley, who was working with me at the time. We looked at each other and I waited to see what she thought. Lesley has a refined palate for buns and I trusted her opinion. She took a bite and looked at me, smiling.

The final and current version of Crumble-Buns is a sweet roll dough, rolled up with granulated sugar in the swirls, then filled with homemade preserves or curd. The buns are piled with a coconut oil crumble, baked, and then drizzled with vanilla glaze. And I think they are perfect.

YOU
DO **YOU**

MAKE THIS

✗ vegan

✗ dairy-free

✗ gluten-free

✗ traditional

YIELD

12 buns

CRUMBLE TOPPING

2 cups (250 g) all-purpose flour or 2 cups gluten-free all-purpose flour

1 cup (200 g) granulated sugar

1 teaspoon pure vanilla extract

¼ teaspoon sea salt

⅓ cup (80 ml) melted coconut oil or butter, or more as needed

BUNS

1 recipe Goldenrod's Favorite Bun Dough of your choice (page 48 or page 51), plus appropriate flour for dusting

4 tablespoons (½ stick, 55 g) unsalted butter or ¼ cup (48 g) vegetable shortening

1 cup (200 g) granulated sugar

1 cup (320 g) jam, preserves (pages 239–241 or store-bought), or lemon curd (page 236 or store-bought) to fill buns

1 recipe Classic Vanilla Glaze (page 221)

Preheat your oven to 375°F and line two baking sheets with parchment paper.

Prepare the crumb topping: Place all the ingredients in a large bowl and stir with a spoon. The mixture should feel fluffy, a little like wet sand, and hold together in small crumble chunks. Add more coconut oil as needed to make the crumble the texture of wet sand. Set aside.

Roll out your choice of dough to a 10-by-20-inch rectangle, keeping the rolling surface lightly floured and moving the dough a little after each roll. You don't want it to stick, and the best way to make sure it isn't sticking is to keep checking. Use more flour as needed.

If you're using the egg-free bun dough, spread your choice of fat over the surface of the dough with a rubber spatula. If you are using the gluten-free bun dough, melt the fat first and brush it on the surface of the dough with a pastry brush. Evenly spread the sugar across the surface of the dough, making sure to get it to every edge and corner. Roll up the dough, starting from a long end and moving up. Make sure it is a tight swirl. Using a sharp chef's knife and working down the length of the roll, cut into 12 2-inch wheels.

Arrange the buns in the prepared pans, about 2 inches apart. We always tuck the tails at Goldenrod. The "tail" is the end of each bun—grab it and fold it under the roll.

This gives each person a really special bit at the bottom of each bun. See the photos on pages 54–57 for a demonstration of this technique.

Let rise in a warm place until the dough is very fluffy to the touch and your finger leaves a slight indentation when you gently poke the edge, about 25 minutes. Press a hole in the center of each bun with your fingers and fill each bun with 2 tablespoons of the filling of your choice. Top each bun with 3 tablespoons of the crumble.

Bake for 30 minutes, until the buns are perfectly golden brown all over and the centers of the each roll do not give back at all when you press them lightly.

Remove from the oven and glaze immediately with Classic Vanilla Glaze, which we dollop on using a #20 scoop, about 3¼ tablespoons (see page 23). Enjoy warm, or within the next 24 hours.

Angela Says

✳ Roll out gluten-free dough on a very well-floured piece of parchment paper or silicone mat. This prevents the dough from losing its structure and will help you to roll out the dough to the correct size. If the dough feels fragile after the filling has been spread, use the parchment paper or mat to roll up the dough. Simply lift the paper with both hands and use it to roll the dough forward, instead of using your hands. Keep going until it's fully rolled.

✳ Use the crumble topping on muffins and pound cakes, as well as The Original Crumble-Bun and Peach Coffee Cake (page 71). This is my version of what I remember from both my mom and my Baba.

✳ If you are making a gluten-free version of the crumble topping, I recommend King Arthur Flour Gluten Free Measure for Measure Flour (240 g) or Nu Life Always Gluten Free All-Purpose Flour (270 g).

FLUFFERNUTTER BUNS

As a teen, learning that you could actually put marshmallow fluff on a sandwich was a game changer for me—I remember asking my friend to ship me a container of fluff when I was studying abroad in Poland! This recipe is based on that old-fashioned fluffernutter: creamy peanut butter and marshmallow fluff sandwiched between two pieces of squishy white bread.

Our fluffernutter is a beautiful swirled bun, filled with creamy peanut butter and brown sugar. It's a love song to all things gooey and perfect. It's glazed with Classic Vanilla Glaze right when it comes out of the oven, so it can seep into all of the little crevices this bun has to offer.

YIELD

12 buns

INGREDIENTS

1 recipe Goldenrod's Favorite Bun Dough of your choice (page 48 or page 51), plus appropriate flour for dusting

1 cup (250 g) creamy peanut butter

½ cup (89 g) light brown sugar

1 recipe Classic Vanilla Glaze (page 221)

Angela Says

✳ We love Jif brand, creamy peanut butter at the bakery for these buns.

✳ Some buns can be glazed a few minutes after they are taken out of the oven, but these buns really need the glaze to be applied immediately after they come out of the oven. The glaze is an important part of the recipe and applying it while the buns are still warm helps it sink into all of the twists and swirls.

Preheat your oven to 400°F and line two baking sheets with a fitted sheet of parchment paper.

Roll out your choice of dough to a 10-by-20-inch rectangle, keeping the rolling surface lightly floured and moving the dough a little after each roll. You don't want it to stick, and the best way to make sure it isn't sticking is to keep checking. Use more flour as needed.

Spread the peanut butter evenly across your dough with a rubber spatula, working carefully so the dough doesn't tear. Make sure the peanut butter reaches every edge and corner. Evenly sprinkle the brown sugar across the peanut butter, again making sure it reachs every edge and corner. Roll up the dough, starting from a long end and moving up. Make sure it is a tight swirl. Using a sharp chef's knife and working down the length of the roll, cut the roll into 12 wedges about 1 inch thick at one end and 3 inches thick at the other.

Arrange the buns in the prepared pans, about 2 inches apart. Put into the oven immediately (many buns require a second rise, but these are better without). Bake for 35 minutes, until the buns are perfectly golden brown all over.

Remove from the oven and glaze immediately with Classic Vanilla Glaze, which we dollop on using a #20 scoop, about 3¼ tablespoons (see page 23). Enjoy warm, or within the next 24 hours.

BITTERSWEET CHOCOLATE BUNS

The beauty of the cocoa powder and brown sugar rolled up in this dough, then totally covered in chocolate ganache, is unmatched. This bun is a thing of beauty, meant for those who aren't afraid of a little chocolate on their fingers or around their mouth.

On my husband's rotating list of favorite buns, this is at the top.

YIELD
12 buns

INGREDIENTS

1 recipe Goldenrod's Favorite Bun Dough of your choice (page 48 or page 51), plus appropriate flour for dusting

4 tablespoons (½ stick, 55 g) unsalted butter or ¼ cup (48 g) vegetable shortening

¾ cup (66 g) unsweetened cocoa powder

⅓ cup (59 g) light brown sugar

1 recipe Chocolate Oven Ganache (page 232)

Preheat your oven to 375°F and line a baking sheet with parchment paper.

Roll out your choice of dough to a 10-by-20-inch rectangle, keeping the rolling surface lightly floured and moving the dough a little after each roll. You don't want it to stick, and the best way to make sure it isn't sticking is to keep checking. Use more flour as needed.

If you're using the egg-free bun dough, spread your choice of fat over the surface of the dough with a rubber spatula. If you are using the rich bun dough, melt the fat first and brush it on the surface of the dough with a pastry brush. Evenly spread the cocoa powder and brown sugar across the surface of the dough, making sure to reach every edge and corner. Roll up the dough, starting from a long end and moving up. Make sure it is a tight swirl. Using a sharp chef's knife and working down the length of the roll, cut into 12 1½-inch buns.

Arrange the buns in the prepared pans, about 2 inches apart. We always tuck the tails at Goldenrod. The "tail" is the end of each bun—grab it and fold it under the roll. This gives each person a really special bit at the bottom of each bun. See the photos on pages 54–57 for a demonstration of this technique.

Let rise in a warm place until the dough is very fluffy to the touch and your finger leaves a slight indentation when you gently poke the edge, about 25 minutes. Bake for 30 to 35 minutes, until the buns are perfectly golden brown all over and the centers of each roll do not give back at all when you press them lightly.

Remove from the oven and let cool at room temperature. Scoop the Chocolate Oven Ganache over each bun once the buns have cooled—we use a #20 scoop, about 3¼ tablespoons (see page 23). These are absolutely best served immediately, but they will keep well for up to 24 hours.

Angela Says

✳ Roll out gluten-free dough on a very well-floured piece of parchment paper or silicone mat. This prevents the dough from losing its structure and will help you to roll out the dough to the correct size. If the dough feels fragile after the filling has been spread, use the parchment paper or mat to roll up the dough. Simply lift the paper with both hands and use it to roll the dough forward, instead of using your hands. Keep going until it's fully rolled.

PEACH COFFEE CAKE

I can't tell you how much I love this recipe. It was one of the first things I made and made again until I made it right. My Baba made this for my family on super rare and special occasions, and the only time we were certain to have it was when we got back from a family vacation. She was totally unpredictable about when she made it otherwise. She lived about a 10-minute drive from our house, and we'd get home late from the airport after these vacations, and the kitchen counters and refrigerator would be empty, except for a sheet pan of peach coffee cake, covered in both a layer of wax paper and then a layer of aluminum foil, and a gallon of milk in the fridge. We would stand around the counter and slowly cut thin pieces off the coffee cake, slowly watching each row dwindle away, while pouring glasses of cold milk. It was the most satisfying thing to come home to. It would get all wrapped up after we had snacked to our hearts' content, and then taken back out in the morning. We usually warmed up leftovers in the oven for as many more days as it stuck around (usually only one or two). Reheating it made the center of the coffee cake almost a little softer and gooey in the crumble, and the edges a little crispy. My mom, brother, and I always went for the edges, and my dad and sister always went for the center.

It's a sweet roll dough crust covered with a layer of sliced, canned peaches, topped with a really rich and perfectly sweet vanilla crumble. I've never tried anything else like it, but customers who have fallen in love with it at the bakery usually compare it to a German kuchen. It's not a coffee cake in the traditional American sense, but a coffee cake, nonetheless. I've tried making this with fresh peaches, and fresh peaches that I preserved myself in syrup. Nothing stands up to the original version with store-bought canned peaches.

This coffee cake can be made vegan. My Baba used butter in both the dough and the crumble on top. I thought she would be mortified when she found out I had altered her recipe by taking out her favorite ingredient, butter. But she accepted it. We had a few days to say good-bye to her before she passed away. I show love and communicate through food. In those last days, the one thing I knew how to do was feed the family who spent time around her in the hospital. I brought bakery boxes full of cinnamon rolls and a full pan of my vegan version of her peach coffee cake. This was the last thing she ate before she passed, and I'll never forget that she took a bite and looked at me and nodded with a smile.

YOU

MAKE THIS

✗ vegan

✗ dairy-free

✗ gluten-free

✗ traditional

YIELD

One 12-by-17-inch coffee cake

CAKE

1 recipe Goldenrod's Favorite Bun Dough of your choice (page 48 or page 51), plus appropriate flour for dusting

Nonstick spray for pan

Four 15-ounce (425 g) cans sliced peaches in light syrup, drained completely

1 recipe Crumble Topping from The Original Crumble-Bun (page 64)

Preheat your oven to 350°F and spray a 12-by-17-inch baking pan with nonstick spray.

Roll out your choice of dough on a floured work surface into a rectangle that will fit the inside of your prepared pan. You want it to fit snugly into the pan, with a slightly raised edge all around. Arrange the drained, sliced peaches evenly across the dough. Sprinkle your crumble all over the top, making sure you cover the entire surface area. Let rise in a warm place for about 10 minutes, then transfer to your oven.

Bake for about 50 minutes, until the edges are perfectly golden brown, the crumble is nice and golden, and the center doesn't move when you gently jiggle the pan.

Remove from the oven and let cool at room temperature. Serve warm or at room temperature. Store, covered, at room temperature for up to 4 days. If you have a lot of coffee cake left over, we recommend freezing it and reheating in the oven to enjoy.

BABKA THREE WAYS

I started making babka at the bakery during our first holiday season. I hadn't actually ever eaten this rich, swirly sweet bread before making it, but it sure seemed like something I would like. After reading through lots of recipes and techniques, I decided how I wanted to make ours at Goldenrod.

The slices I had always seen of babka showed an intensely swirled interior and I was worried that mine wouldn't be swirly enough, or that I wouldn't make the correct kind of swirl. But if there is one thing I've learned, it's that all swirls are valid and your babka will be delicious no matter what your swirl looks like. All swirls are special, unique, and delicious.

I am giving you three filling options. Chocolate is most traditional, raspberry is a little lighter, and peanut butter is absolutely not traditional, but was a suggestion from my friends Julie and Brian and it's one of the most delicious treats imaginable.

PERFECTLY GOLDEN

One 9-by-5-inch loaf

DOUGH

2½ cups (312 g) all-purpose flour or 2½ cups gluten-free all-purpose flour, plus appropriate flour for dusting

¾ cup (180 ml) milk, almond milk, or your favorite nondairy milk

¼ cup (50 g) granulated sugar

1 tablespoon active dry yeast

¼ cup (60 ml) vegetable oil

½ teaspoon sea salt

Nonstick spray for pan

FILLING OPTIONS

CHOCOLATE

¾ cup (68 g) unsweetened cocoa powder

½ cup (89 g) light brown sugar

½ cup (120 ml) melted coconut oil

RASPBERRY

½ cup (120 ml) melted coconut oil

1½ cups (200 g) fresh raspberries

½ cup (100 g) granulated sugar

PEANUT BUTTER

¾ cup (190 g) creamy peanut butter

¼ cup (45 g) light brown sugar

GLAZE

1 recipe Classic Vanilla Glaze (page 221) or 1 recipe Chocolate Oven Ganache (page 232)

Angela Says

✳ For the gluten-free flour, I recommend Pamela's Gluten-Free All-Purpose Flour (300 g).

Bloom the yeast: Heat your milk to about 110°F. Any hotter and you will kill your yeast; much cooler and your yeast will take a very long time to activate. It should be warm to the touch. Pour the warm milk into a large bowl and add your sugar and yeast. Use a handheld whisk to combine. I like to set the bowl on top of a preheating oven to bloom, but your counter is fine, too.

This takes about 10 minutes. The yeast is ready when the mixture looks foamy on top.

Mix the dough: Add the oil, salt, and flour to the bowl and use a wooden spoon to combine the ingredients into as much of a cohesive mass as possible. If you are using traditional flour, once mostly combined, turn the dough out onto a lightly floured counter and knead by hand for about 10 minutes, until the dough becomes a smooth, supple, soft ball. If you are using gluten-free flour, there is no need to knead your dough.

If using traditional flour dough, transfer the dough back to the mixing bowl and let it rise in a warm place for about 40 minutes, or until it has doubled in size. Gluten-free dough, it rises fairly quickly so does not need to be set aside to rise.

Assemble the babka: Spray a 9-by-5-inch loaf pan with nonstick spray. Once your dough has risen and is very soft and impossibly fluffy, roll out to an 8-by-14-inch rectangle on a floured work surface. Spread with your filling of choice. The chocolate filling should be slightly warm to be spreadable. For the raspberry filling, spread the melted coconut oil on the rolled dough, then sprinkle with the raspberries and sugar. For a peanut butter babka, spread the peanut butter gently over the rolled dough, then sprinkle with the brown sugar. Make sure the filling reaches every edge and corner.

Roll up the dough starting from a long side and moving up. Make sure it is a tight swirl. Using a sharp chef's knife, cut directly down the length of the roll, keeping one end intact. Working with confidence, twist the two strands of swirled dough, one over the other. This may look messy at this point, but I promise, it will be great.

Lift the twisted dough by each end and transfer to your prepared loaf pan. You will have to greatly condense the long, twisted dough to fit in the loaf pan—it will make a tall, voluptuous-looking babka, which is, of course, what we want.

Bake the babka: Preheat your oven to 350°F. Let the babka rise for about 30 minutes in a warm place. It should increase in volume and should feel very soft to the touch when gently pressed with your finger. Bake for approximately 30 minutes, until the outside is dark golden brown and the middle of the babka does not give back at all when gently pressed. To be sure the dough is fully baked, you can check to be sure the temperature reads 190°F on a thermometer inserted into the center of the bread.

Remove from the oven and let cool at room temperature. Finish with your choice of glaze, drizzled over the top of the loaf. Enjoy immediately, or cover and store at room temperature for up to 2 days.

COOKIES

The bakers at Goldenrod take a lot of pride in their perfectly baked cookies. Every tray that comes out of the oven with perfectly golden-brown edges and soft, barely gooey centers feels like a personal accomplishment. But we even like the imperfect cookies more because, as my mom always called them when we were growing up, "employee cookies" are always the best.

There's nothing too fancy about these cookies. But that's what we love about cookies, isn't it? Present a big pile of them to a group, and everyone rushes to get the cookie that looks perfect to them. Wrap them up and throw a few in your purse or your pocket! In my life and at Goldenrod, I firmly believe that a few cookie crumbs at the bottom of your pocket means you are doing something right. Grab it and go, a cookie is the perfect snack.

Some of my favorite memories are around a mixing bowl of cookie dough with my family, or around a tray of freshly baked cookies with my friends. And at Goldenrod, we crowd around the plates of employee cookies with that same joy.

It was difficult for me not to say that every cookie in this book is my favorite. I love them all.

BASE COOKIE + VARIATIONS

This recipe is endlessly customizable. Just keep in mind that you will significantly change the recipe if you add additional liquid or a dry ingredient, such as cocoa powder, or ground nuts. What you can do is add new flavors in the form of dried fruit, flavored extracts, spices, whole nuts, additional chocolate pieces, or citrus zests.

YIELD

20 to 24 cookies

Angela Says

✴ For the gluten-free flour, I recommend Nu Life Always Gluten Free All-Purpose Flour (371 g) or King Arthur Gluten Free Measure for Measure Flour (330 g).

✴ You can freeze the dough after you portion it into cookie dough balls. If you bake them directly from the freezer, add 3 minutes to the total baking time. After the first 7 minutes of baking, we like to use a piece of parchment paper to gently press down each cookie.

✴ The cookie dough texture should always feel about the same: you want it to look a little fluffy, but when you insert a spoon, the dough shouldn't be wet enough to coat your utensil. Soft, but not sticky!

BASE

½ pound (2 sticks, 225 g) unsalted butter, at room temperature, or 1 cup (192 g) vegetable shortening

2 cups (400 g) granulated sugar

½ cup (89 g) light brown sugar

1 teaspoon pure vanilla extract

2 large eggs or flax eggs (page 30)

1 teaspoon baking soda

½ teaspoon sea salt

2¾ cups (344 g) all-purpose flour or 2¾ cups gluten-free all-purpose flour

Preheat your oven to 375°F and line two baking sheets with parchment paper.

Combine your choice of fat, ½ cup (100 g) of the granulated sugar, the brown sugar, and the vanilla in the bowl of a stand mixer fitted with the paddle attachment and mix on medium-high speed for about 5 minutes, adding one egg at a time. The mixture should be homogeneous and fluffy. Add the baking soda, salt, and flour and mix on low speed to incorporate. It's important to make sure the cookie dough is well mixed, so be sure to stir it again once you have taken the bowl away from the stand mixer. Fold from the bottom of the bowl to the top, getting everything evenly mixed.

We use the #24 scoop for our cookies, about 2¾ tablespoons (see page 41). You can also scoop the dough with a large soup spoon. Roll cookies in the remaining 1½ cups (329 g) of granulated sugar. Place about 2 inches apart on the prepared baking sheets. Press down each cookie gently with the palm of your hand or the bottom of a drinking glass. Bake for about 12 minutes, or until the edges of the cookies are set and the center feels soft to the touch.

Remove from the oven and let cool completely on the baking sheets or transfer carefully to cooling racks. These will keep really well at room temperature, in an airtight container, for about a week.

COOKIE VARIATIONS

CONFETTI SPRINKLE

Substitute ½ cup (100 g) of granulated sugar for the brown sugar in the Base Cookie recipe, so you will have 1 cup (200 g) of granulated sugar total. Add 1 teaspoon of pure vanilla extract or almond extract (go with vanilla for almond-free) to the mixture, depending on your preference.

Roll the cookies in 1 to 2 cups (160 to 320 g) of rainbow or solid-colored jimmy sprinkles (dairy- or gluten-free, if necessary). Yes, this is a lot of sprinkles—but the effect of a rainbow-covered cookie is totally worth it! Press down the cookie dough balls slightly with the palm of your hand or the bottom of a glass before baking.

TRAIL MIX

Add the zest of 2 oranges to the fat and sugar at the beginning of the recipe. Once the dough has come together, fold in 1 cup (about 150 g) of your favorite trail mix blend (dairy-, gluten-, and/or nut-free, if necessary) and ½ cup (50 g) of sweetened shredded coconut. Press down the cookie dough balls slightly with the palm of your hand or the bottom of a glass before baking.

OATMEAL RAISIN

Substitute ½ cup (89 g) of light brown sugar for the initial ½ cup (100 g) of granulated sugar in the beginning of the recipe, so you will have 1 cup (179 g) of brown sugar total. Add an additional ¼ teaspoon of sea salt, and ½ teaspoon of ground cinnamon. You will also need 1¾ cups (157 g) of rolled oats (certified gluten-free, if necessary) and 1¼ cups (200 g) of raisins. Press down the cookie dough balls slightly with the palm of your hand or the bottom of a glass before baking.

CHOCOLATE CHIP COOKIES

Full disclosure: chocolate chip cookies have always been my least favorite cookie. But, through a few changes to the recipe and our special Goldenrod baking method, I have really grown to love them. The sorghum-based gluten-free flour that we use in this, and in most of our cookies, makes a really tender cookie. The cookies have an almost flaky texture straight out of the oven and continue to have over the next 48 hours after baking. Sorghum has an almost nutty flavor that captures some of the sweetness, making the final product not too sweet at all. This is a great example of how nontraditional ingredients can actually improve the overall product! The smear of melted chocolate across the top of each cookie is our signature look.

This is a classic and I'm really proud of this recipe we use at Goldenrod.

YOU DO YOU
MAKE THIS
- ✗ vegan
- ✗ dairy-free
- ✗ gluten-free
- ✗ traditional

YIELD
20 to 24 cookies

Angela Says

✳ For the gluten-free flour, I recommend Nu Life Always Gluten Free All-Purpose Flour (270 g) or King Arthur Gluten Free Measure for Measure Flour (240 g).

✳ Make these in advance and freeze the cookie dough balls. Stored in an airtight container, these will last in the freezer for about 2 months. Bake directly from frozen and press down with the bottom of a glass about 6 minutes through the baking process. You'll add about 5 minutes to the baking time when you bake from frozen.

✳ Roll the cookie dough in raw sugar for a little more texture and sparkle on the finished product.

INGREDIENTS

½ pound (2 sticks, 225 g) unsalted butter, at room temperature, or 1 cup (192 g) vegetable shortening

½ cup (100 g) granulated sugar

½ cup (89 g) light brown sugar

1 teaspoon pure vanilla extract

2 large eggs or flax eggs (page 30)

1 teaspoon baking soda

½ teaspoon sea salt

2 cups (250 g) all-purpose flour or 2 cups gluten-free all-purpose flour

1 cup (155 g) bittersweet chocolate chips, vegan if necessary

---

Preheat your oven to 375°F and line two baking sheets with parchment paper.

Combine your choice of fat with the granulated sugar, brown sugar, and vanilla in the bowl of stand mixer fitted with the paddle attachment and mix on medium-high speed for about 5 minutes, adding one egg at a time. The mixture should be homogeneous and fluffy. Add the baking soda, salt, and flour and mix on low speed to incorporate. Finally, pour in the chocolate chips and mix briefly with the mixer to incorporate them. It's important to make sure the cookie dough is well mixed, so be sure to stir it again once you have taken the bowl away from the stand mixer. Fold from the bottom of the bowl to the top, getting everything evenly mixed.

We use the #24 scoop for our cookies, about 2¾ tablespoons (see page 41). You can also scoop the dough with a large soup spoon. Place 2 inches apart on the prepared baking sheets. Bake for about 12 minutes, or until the edges of the cookies are set and the center feels soft to the touch. About halfway through the baking process, gently press down the cookies with either a piece of parchment paper or the bottom of a glass. This flattens the cookies slightly to give them a nice even top, and also smashes the melted chocolate chips.

Remove from the oven and let cool completely on the baking sheets or transfer carefully to cooling racks. These will keep really well at room temperature, in an airtight container, for about a week.

DOUBLE CHOCOLATE COOKIES

YOU
DO **YOU**

MAKE THIS

✗ vegan

✗ dairy-free

✗ gluten-free

✗ traditional

At the time of writing this book, this cookie really is my favorite cookie. And I wait patiently to see if any will fall victim to breaking on the baking sheet, or when being transferred to a cake stand to sit atop the pastry case—because I crave this cookie. I think about it so often, and this is coming from a person who does not seek out chocolate, nor do I usually want chocolate chips in my cookies. This is one of my "never say never" moments—because this cookie is truly divine.

YIELD
20 to 24 cookies

INGREDIENTS

½ pound (2 sticks, 225 g) unsalted butter, at room temperature, or 1 cup (192 g) vegetable shortening

1 cup (179 g) light brown sugar

2 large eggs or flax eggs (page 30)

1 teaspoon pure vanilla extract

1 teaspoon sea salt

1 teaspoon baking soda

⅓ cup (30 g) unsweetened cocoa powder

2 cups (200 g) all-purpose flour or 2 cups gluten-free all-purpose flour

2 cups (310 g) bittersweet chocolate chips, vegan if necessary

Preheat your oven to 375°F and line two baking sheets with parchment paper.

Combine your choice of fat with the brown sugar and vanilla in the bowl of a stand mixer fitted with the paddle attachment and mix on medium-high speed for about 5 minutes, adding one egg at a time. The mixture should be homogeneous and fluffy. Add the baking soda, salt, cocoa powder, and flour and mix on low speed to incorporate. Finally, pour in the chocolate chips and mix briefly with the mixer to integrate. It's important to make sure the cookie dough is well mixed, so be sure to stir it again once you have taken the bowl away from the stand mixer. Fold from the bottom of the bowl to the top, getting everything evenly mixed.

We use the #24 scoop for our cookies, about 2¾ table-spoons (see page 41). You can also scoop the dough with a large soup spoon. Place 2 inches apart on the prepared baking sheets. Bake for about 12 minutes, or until the edges of the cookies are set and the center feels soft to the touch. About halfway through the baking process, gently press down the cookies with either a piece of parchment paper or the bottom of a glass. This flattens the cookies slightly to give them a nice even top, and also smashes the melted chocolate chips.

Remove from the oven and let cool completely on the baking sheets or transfer carefully to cooling racks. These will keep really well at room temperature, in an airtight container, for about a week.

Angela Says

✳ For the gluten-free flour, I recommend Nu Life Always Gluten Free All-Purpose Flour (270 g) or King Arthur Gluten Free Measure for Measure Flour (240 g).

✳ Because these cookies have a dark chocolate color, it's easy to overbake them. Don't wait to take them out of the oven until they look darker, just make sure the center of the cookie looks matte, and the edge of the cookie is firm to the touch.

SOFT MOLASSES COOKIES

I spend most of the summer at the bakery trying to convince my team of bakers that chewy molasses cookies are a good all-year-round cookie and shouldn't be left just to the fall and winter. They get the most delicious sugary cookie crust on the outside, but stay totally cakey and chewy in the middle. This recipe took longer to develop than some others, because of the added moisture from the molasses. But what we get from that is a super dark, delicious flavor and an incredibly decadent texture.

Be like me, and make these any time of the year!

YIELD
20 to 24 cookies

Angela Says

✳ For the gluten-free flour, I recommend Nu Life Always Gluten Free All-Purpose Flour (540 g) or King Arthur Gluten Free Measure for Measure Flour (480 g).

✳ Make these in advance and freeze the sugar-coated cookie dough balls. Stored in an airtight container, these will last in the freezer for about two months. Bake directly from frozen!

✳ Molasses lends itself well to lots of spice, so add your favorites. You can add up to 2 more teaspoons of spice, but divide it between ground dried spices, such as cinnamon, cardamom, nutmeg, and allspice.

INGREDIENTS

½ pound (2 sticks, 225 g) unsalted butter, at room temperature, or 1 cup (192 g) vegetable shortening

1 cup (179 g) light brown sugar

2 large eggs or flax eggs (page 30)

½ cup (147 g) blackstrap molasses

1 teaspoon baking soda

½ teaspoon sea salt

1 teaspoon ground ginger

1 teaspoon grated fresh ginger (optional)

4 cups (500 g) all-purpose flour or 4 cups gluten-free all-purpose flour

¾ cup (150 g) granulated sugar for rolling cookies

Preheat your oven to 400°F and line two baking sheets with parchment paper.

Combine your choice of fat with the brown sugar, eggs, and molasses in the bowl of a stand mixer fitted with the paddle attachment and mix on medium-high speed for about 5 minutes, or until the mixture is homogeneous and fluffy. Add the baking soda, salt, ground ginger, grated ginger (if using), and flour and mix on low speed to incorporate. It's important to make sure the cookie dough is well mixed, so be sure to stir it again once you have taken the bowl away from the stand mixer. Fold from the bottom of the bowl to the top, getting everything evenly mixed.

We use the #24 scoop for our cookies, about 2¾ tablespoons (see page 41). You can also scoop the dough with a large soup spoon. Roll the cookies in the granulated sugar. Place about 2 inches apart on the prepared baking sheets. Bake for about 12 minutes, or until the edges of the cookies are set and the center feels soft to the touch. About halfway through the baking process, gently press down the cookies with either a piece of parchment paper or the bottom of a glass. This flattens the cookies slightly to give them a nice even top.

Remove from the oven and let cool completely on the baking sheets before transferring to a plate or serving dish. These will keep really well at room temperature, in an airtight container, for about a week.

PEANUT BUTTER COOKIES

Peanut butter cookies have always been completely irresistible to me. It is essential to have the outside rolled in granulated sugar, to have the inside be a little cakey and incredibly soft, and you absolutely can't forget a healthy dose of salt. I always sneak back into the kitchen to grab another bite of this cookie. Thinking I'll only eat one is always a mistake.

We use a fork to crosshatch the top of each cookie for a little extra texture and a totally nostalgic look.

YOU DO YOU

MAKE THIS

X vegan
X dairy-free
X gluten-free
X traditional

YIELD

20 to 24 cookies

INGREDIENTS

½ cup (125 g) creamy peanut butter

½ pound (2 sticks, 225 g) unsalted butter, at room temperature, or 1 cup (192 g) vegetable shortening

½ cup (89 g) light brown sugar

½ cup (100 g) granulated sugar, plus ¾ cup (150 g) for rolling

2 large eggs or flax eggs (page 30)

1 teaspoon pure vanilla extract

½ teaspoon baking soda

1 teaspoon sea salt

2 cups (250 g) all-purpose flour or 2 cups gluten-free all-purpose flour

Angela Says

* We love Jif brand creamy peanut butter at the bakery for these cookies.

* For the gluten-free flour, I recommend Nu Life Always Gluten Free All-Purpose Flour (270 g) or King Arthur Gluten Free Measure for Measure Flour (240 g).

* Make these in advance and freeze the sugar-coated cookie dough balls. Stored in an airtight container, these will last in the freezer for about 2 months. Bake directly from frozen!

* Roll the peanut butter cookie dough in raw sugar for a little more texture and sparkle on the finished product.

* One of the keys to a fluffy and delicious cookie is making sure the fat, sugar, and eggs are well mixed. Scrape down the bowl as often as necessary during that first mixing step to be sure the mixture is evenly blended.

Preheat your oven to 375°F and line two baking sheets with parchment paper.

Combine the peanut butter, your choice of fat, the brown sugar, ½ cup (100 g) of the granulated sugar, and the vanilla in the bowl of a stand mixer fitted with the paddle attachment and mix on medium-high speed for about 5 minutes, adding one egg at a time. The mixture should be homogeneous and fluffy. Add the baking soda, salt, and flour and mix on low speed to incorporate. It's important to make sure the cookie dough is well mixed, so be sure to stir it again once you have taken the bowl away from the stand mixer. Fold from the bottom of the bowl to the top, getting everything evenly mixed.

We use the #24 scoop for our cookies, about 2¾ tablespoons (see page 41). You can also scoop the dough with a large soup spoon. Roll the cookies in the remaining ¾ cup (150 g) of granulated sugar. Place about 2 inches apart on the prepared baking sheets and press the top of each cookie with the back of a fork. Bake for about 12 minutes, or until the edges of the cookie are set and the center feels soft to the touch. Because these cookies are darker in color from the peanut butter, it is hard to judge their doneness based on color, so you have to rely on touch for these!

Remove from the oven and let cool completely on the baking sheets before transferring to a plate or serving dish. These will keep really well at room temperature, in an airtight container, for about a week.

TURTLE COOKIES

I asked my mom for permission to tweak and share her recipe—and she said, "As long as it is making someone happy, I'm always happy to share a recipe." So, with that sentiment, I am sharing one of my family's all-time favorite cookie recipes. The little brownie-like dollops of cookie dough are baked in a traditional waffle iron for a few seconds, then topped with peanut butter frosting. They are popular all year-round, but we always enjoyed them especially in the summer, when my mom didn't want to heat up the house by turning on the oven. Her waffle iron is about 40 years old, incredibly rickety, but still heats up well and is perfect to make dozens of little waffle cookies, better known as turtle cookies. My best friend, Ashley, would always request them when she came home from college, or asked me to bring some whenever I visited. They bake just a few at a time, and my siblings and I would crowd around the kitchen island, eagerly waiting for my mom to pull them out of the waffle iron, let them cool on sheets of wax paper, and then top each one with a butter knife piled with peanut butter frosting.

Simply put, these are delightful.

The best waffle irons for this use have the word *classic* in the name—they're typically used to make thin, crispy waffles.

YOU DO **YOU**

MAKE THIS

- ✗ vegan
- ✗ dairy-free
- ✗ gluten-free
- ✗ traditional

YIELD

20 to 24 cookies

COOKIES

1 cup (200 g) granulated sugar

3 large eggs or flax eggs (page 30)

¾ cup (180 ml) melted coconut oil

1½ teaspoons pure vanilla extract

½ cup (45 g) unsweetened cocoa powder

½ teaspoon sea salt

1½ cups (188 g) all-purpose flour or 1½ cups gluten-free all-purpose flour

Nonstick spray for waffle iron

PEANUT BUTTER FROSTING

3 cups (360 g) powdered sugar

¼ cup (65 g) creamy peanut butter

2 to 3 tablespoons milk, almond milk, or your favorite nondairy milk

1 teaspoon pure vanilla extract

½ teaspoon sea salt

Preheat your waffle iron to the medium-high setting according to the manufacturer's instructions.

Prepare the cookies: Whisk together the sugar, eggs, coconut oil, and vanilla in a large bowl. Once the mixture comes together, add the cocoa powder, salt, and flour and mix together gently with a rubber spatula or wooden spoon.

Spray the inside of the waffle iron with nonstick spray before each new batch of cookies goes in. Drop 1-teaspoon spoonfuls of batter into the iron, spacing the cookies about 2 inches apart. Each waffle iron will be different, but the cookies should bake for 45 to 60 seconds. Gently remove the cookies with a fork and allow to cool. Although my mom always let these cool on sheets of wax paper laid directly on the counter, you are welcome to let the cookies cool on baking sheets, a cooling rack, or pieces of parchment paper. Continue to bake the cookies in batches and prepare the frosting while they cool.

Prepare the frosting: Stir together the powdered sugar and peanut butter in a small bowl, using a fork. Add the milk, vanilla, and salt and mix with the fork to incorporate.

Frost the top of each cooled cookie with peanut butter frosting. Serve immediately, or store in an airtight container at room temperature for up to 1 week.

Angela Says

✱ For the gluten-free flour, I recommend Nu Life Always Gluten Free All-Purpose Flour (203 g) or King Arthur Gluten Free Measure for Measure Flour (180 g).

✱ You can also bake these in the oven, preheated to 375°F, on a greased baking sheet for 12 minutes.

BUCKWHEAT CHOCOLATE CHUNK COOKIES

This is a revolutionary cookie. It's a cookie that defines Goldenrod to me—taking a classic like the chocolate chip cookie, and making it better by bringing out the earthy notes in buckwheat. I usually try to take the straightforward approach to things, such as using chocolate chips instead of chopping chocolate for recipes, but I love the effect chopped chocolate has in this cookie. Not only do you get the actual chunks of chocolate, but you end up with a spray of chocolate dust that becomes one with the dough. The buckwheat flour and chocolate dust become almost indistinguishable from one another. It's perfectly chewy and everything you want from a cookie.

YIELD
20 to 24 cookies

Angela Says

✳ For the gluten-free flour, I recommend Nu Life Always Gluten Free All-Purpose Flour (169 g) or King Arthur Gluten Free Measure for Measure Flour (150 g).

✳ These cookies are great without chocolate, too. If you don't live for chocolate, or are looking for a more neutral cookie, try making them without chocolate.

✳ Make a batch of our Chocolate Oven Ganache (page 232) and dip the tops of the finished, cooled cookies into it. This adds a really luxurious touch and takes the cookies to the next level for a more formal event.

INGREDIENTS

1⅓ cups (237 g)
light brown sugar

¼ cup (30 g)
cornstarch, potato starch, or tapioca starch

⅔ cup (160 ml) melted coconut oil

½ cup (120 ml) milk, almond milk, or your favorite nondairy milk

1 teaspoon
pure vanilla extract

½ teaspoon baking soda

1 teaspoon baking powder

1 teaspoon sea salt

1¾ cups (250 g)
buckwheat flour

1¼ cups (156 g) all-purpose flour or 1¼ cups gluten-free all-purpose flour

1½ cups (232 g) chopped bittersweet chocolate, vegan if necessary

Preheat your oven to 350°F and line two baking sheets with parchment paper.

Combine the brown sugar, cornstarch, coconut oil, milk, and vanilla extract in a medium bowl. Whisk together vigorously until the mixture looks creamy and smooth, about a minute or two. Add the baking soda and baking powder, salt, buckwheat flour, and all-purpose flour. Fold together with a rubber spatula until combined. Add the chocolate chunks and any chocolate dust left from chopping, and fold into the dough.

We use the #24 scoop for our cookies, about 2¾ tablespoons (see page 41). You can also scoop the dough with a large soup spoon. Place the cookies about 2 inches apart on the prepared baking sheets. Press down each cookie gently with the palm of your hand or the bottom of a glass. Bake for about 12 minutes, or until the edges of the cookies are set and the center feels soft to the touch. Because these cookies are darker in color from the buckwheat flour, it is hard to judge their doneness based on color, so you have to rely on touch for these!

Remove from the oven and let cool completely on the baking sheets or transfer carefully to cooling racks. These will keep really well at room temperature, in an airtight container, for about a week.

COCONUT BERRY THUMBPRINT COOKIES

I attended an arts-focused high school. Most of my classmates painted, did photography, worked with clay, or even wrote poetry and novels. I didn't fall in any of those categories and always wondered why I felt I fit in so well with the artist crowd, but felt a little left out when the school's art show came up and I didn't know what I would contribute. A teacher asked me whether I would want to bake for the show. It was the first time someone had called out baking as my craft and my art. That was a turning point for me and helped me come into my own as a creative, through my craft: baking.

I kept a three-ring binder bursting with recipes in the rings, in the pockets, and with pages stuffed in when those were all full. This cookie was one of the first recipes in that binder. It's an incredible shortbread, coated in shredded coconut, and filled with preserves. I made this recipe for my first catering event as a baker, when I was 17.

YIELD
20 to 24 cookies

INGREDIENTS

¾ pound (3 sticks, 338 g) unsalted butter, at room temperature, or 1½ cups (288 g) vegetable shortening

1 cup (200 g) granulated sugar

2 teaspoons pure vanilla extract

½ teaspoon sea salt

3½ cups (438 g) all-purpose flour or 3½ cups gluten-free all-purpose flour

2 cups (205 g) shredded sweetened coconut

1 cup (320 g) jam, preserves (page 239–241 or store-bought), or lemon curd (page 236 or store-bought)

Preheat your oven to 375°F and line two baking sheets with parchment paper.

Combine your choice of fat with the sugar, vanilla, and salt in the bowl of a stand mixer fitted with a paddle attachment and cream until light and fluffy, about 3 minutes on medium-high speed. Add the flour and mix to incorporate. Place the shredded coconut in a small bowl. Scoop the cookie dough in 2-tablespoon balls (#30 scoop and roll in the coconut, pressing lightly to make sure it sticks to the dough.

Place the cookies about 2 inches apart on the prepared baking sheets. Use your thumb to gently make an indentation in the middle of each cookie. Use a small spoon to drop ½ teaspoon of preserves into the center of each cookie indentation.

Bake for about 15 minutes until the coconut is a medium brown color and the cookies do not give when you press them lightly with your finger.

Remove from the oven and let cool completely on the baking sheet or transfer carefully to cooling racks before transferring to a plate or serving dish. These will keep really well at room temperature, in an airtight container, for about a week.

Angela Says

✳ For the gluten-free flour, I recommend Nu Life Always Gluten Free All-Purpose Flour (473 g) or King Arthur Gluten Free Measure for Measure Flour (420 g).

✳ You can use any flavor of jam, preserves, or curd in the center of these cookies. We have used raspberry preserves, blueberry jam, mixed berry preserves, and lemon curd.

OLD SCHOOL PEANUT BUTTER COOKIE SANDWICHES

YOU
DO YOU

MAKE THIS

✗ vegan
✗ dairy-free
✗ gluten-free
✗ traditional

This was our original cookie sandwich at Goldenrod. I was still figuring out a really successful way to make delicious gluten-free cookies and learned about making peanut butter cookies completely without flour. I knew this would be a good place to start while I continued learning and figuring out how to make the best gluten-free cookie recipe (see Goldenrod's Favorite Peanut Butter Cookie, page 84). It's so simple and tender—and was just begging for a healthy swirl of chocolate buttercream. So, the Old School Peanut Butter Cookie Sandwich was born!

We tried taking this off the menu once. Never again. People revolted. It will never leave again.

YIELD

24 cookies, 12 cookie sandwiches

INGREDIENTS

2 cups (500 g) creamy peanut butter

2 large eggs or flax eggs (page 30)

1½ cups (300 g) granulated sugar

1 teaspoon sea salt

1½ teaspoons baking soda

1 recipe Dark Chocolate Buttercream (page 225)

Preheat your oven to 375°F and line two baking sheets with parchment paper.

Combine the peanut butter, eggs, sugar, salt, and baking soda in a medium bowl and fold together all the ingredients with a rubber spatula. The dough is ready when the ingredients are evenly combined and you don't see any streaks of egg or pure peanut butter running through the mix.

We use the #20 scoop for these cookies, about 2 tablespoons (see page 41). You can also scoop the dough with a small soup spoon. Place the cookies about 2 inches apart on the prepared baking sheets. Press down each cookie gently with the palm of your hand or the bottom of a drinking glass. Bake for about 12 minutes, or until the edges of the cookie are set and the center feels soft to the touch. Because these cookies are darker in color from the peanut butter, it is hard to judge their doneness based on color, so you have to rely on touch for these!

Remove from the oven and let the cookies cool completely on the cookie sheets. Flip over half of them to add a swirl of Dark Chocolate Buttercream, and create a sandwich with the rest of the cookies.

Angela Says

* Make sure not to overmix this cookie dough. It's done mixing when the ingredients are *just* combined. Overmixed cookies are still delicious, but the shape gets a little shaggy.

CHEWY ALMOND COOKIES

YOU
DO YOU

MAKE THIS

☐ vegan

✗ dairy-free

✗ gluten-free

✗ traditional

These are really humble-looking cookies but once people try them, they can't resist the slightly crunchy-chewy edge and crust that surrounds the fluffy, light, slightly sweet almond center.

With only three ingredients, these cookies come together really quickly. At the bakery, our favorite way to eat them is dipped in any leftover chocolate ganache. You might even make a batch of ganache especially for the occasion (see Chocolate Oven Ganache, page 232).

YIELD

15 to 20 cookies

INGREDIENTS

5 large egg whites

1½ cups (300 g) granulated sugar

4½ cups (432 g) almond flour

Preheat your oven to 350°F and line two baking sheets with parchment paper.

You can mix these cookies with a stand mixer or by hand. Whisk the egg whites until they form stiff peaks. Add the sugar and almond flour. If you're using a stand mixer, whisk in the sugar and almond flour with the mixer. If you are mixing by hand, fold in the sugar and almond flour.

We recommend using the #20 scoop for these cookies, about 3¼ tablespoons (see page 41). You can also scoop the dough with a large soup spoon. Place the cookies about 2 inches apart on the prepared baking sheets. Bake for 25 minutes, or until the entire cookie is golden brown and just barely soft to the touch when you gently press on the top.

Remove from the oven and let cool completely on the baking sheets before transferring to a storage container or serving tray. These adhere to the parchment paper a little during baking, so you need to wait until they are fully cool to transfer.

ALMOND BISCOTTI

When I was a teenager, this was a recipe I made often. Biscotti had a pretty strong moment in the late '90s and early 2000s, but seem to have fallen out of favor. My biscotti are specifically designed to be dipped in hot coffee. While delicious on their own, their flavor is heightened and the almond really comes out with coffee. If you use the gluten-free flour option, it tenderizes the cookie in a beautiful way. The sharpness and crunch of biscotti is still there, but you won't break your teeth!

   Biscotti are twice-baked cookies: you will make the dough into a loaf shape, bake that fully, then slice that loaf into the traditional biscotti shape we are used to, and bake it again. This cookie was originally made for the function of being very dry, which meant it could be stored for long periods of time in an era that didn't have refrigeration. You won't have to worry about that with this recipe because it will disappear too fast.

YOU
DO YOU

MAKE THIS

✗ vegan

✗ dairy-free

✗ gluten-free

✗ traditional

INGREDIENTS

1 cup (110 g) sliced almonds

8 tablespoons (1 stick, 112 g) unsalted butter, at room temperature, or ½ cup (96 g) vegetable shortening

1 cup (200 g) granulated sugar

3 large eggs or flax eggs (page 30)

1 teaspoon almond extract

1 teaspoon pure vanilla extract

4 teaspoons brandy (optional)

1½ teaspoons baking powder

1½ teaspoons sea salt

3 cups (375 g) all-purpose flour or 3 cups gluten-free all-purpose flour

Preheat your oven to 350°F and line a baking sheet with parchment paper.

Spread the sliced almonds on the prepared pan and toast in the oven for about 10 minutes, or until they have a nice nutty aroma and are golden brown. Remove from the oven and set aside to cool.

Add the fat of your choice and the granulated sugar in the bowl of a stand mixer fitted with the paddle attachment and mix on medium speed just to combine. Then start adding in the eggs, one at a time, mixing to incorporate after each egg addition. Increase the speed to medium-high and beat for about 2 minutes, or until the mixture is light and fluffy. Add the almond extract, brandy (if using), baking powder, salt, and flour. Mix to combine.

Form the dough into a roughly 12-by-4-inch rectangular loaf on the prepared baking sheet. Bake for about 40 minutes, or until the loaf is golden brown and doesn't give back at all when you gently touch the center. Set aside to cool completely.

Remove from the oven and let cool on the pan. Once cool, use a sharp serrated knife and gently cut 1-inch-thick slices. I like to cut along the diagonal, which makes a more dramatic biscotti shape. Be sure you are slicing with the knife moving back and forth across the loaf—if you just press down directly through the loaf, it will crush the biscotti, as opposed to making nice slices.

Place the biscotti slices back on their original baking sheet. Because they are already baked, you don't need to worry about these spreading; they can be about 1 inch apart. Bake for 12 minutes, then gently flip the biscotti and bake for another 10 minutes.

Remove from the oven and let cool completely before serving or storing. These will last for about 3 weeks at room temperature in an airtight storage container, or about 3 months frozen.

Angela Says

✱ For the gluten-free flour, I recommend Nu Life Always Gluten Free All-Purpose Flour (405 g) or King Arthur Gluten Free Measure for Measure Flour (360 g).

✱ You can alter the flavors in this recipe by omitting the almonds, extract, and brandy. If you omit that liquid, just replace with another flavored liquid you like, or a little almond milk to balance out the texture of the dough. One example would be: use 1 tablespoon of rose water to replace the almond extract, add 1 cup (124 g) of chopped pistachios to replace the almonds, and replace the brandy with 3 tablespoons of water. Lemon juice would be another great brandy replacement.

PECAN SHORTBREAD COOKIES

It's hard to find a cookie that isn't too sweet and that you can eat at any time of day. We started making these pecan shortbread cookies as little cut-out people and couldn't resist adding indented button marks. The richness of the pecans is a welcome, nutty fattiness that you can't get any other way. I make this as a holiday cookie because it does take a little extra time to roll and cut them out, plus the pecans are a bit of a bigger purchase. These cookies are for when you want to splurge and have time to spend a little longer on making treats.

Feel free to bake these in a different shape; just make sure the shape is 3 inches across or smaller. Any bigger and the outside of the cookie will get a little too brown before the center is fully baked.

YOU DO YOU

MAKE THIS

✗ vegan
✗ dairy-free
✗ gluten-free
✗ traditional

YIELD

25 to 30 cookies

INGREDIENTS

1 cup (100 g) pecans

2¼ cups (281 g) all-purpose flour or 2¼ cups gluten-free all-purpose flour, plus appropriate flour, for dusting

12 tablespoons (1½ sticks, 167 g) unsalted butter or ¾ cups (144 g) vegetable shortening

2 tablespoons powdered sugar

1 teaspoon pure vanilla extract

¼ teaspoon sea salt

⅓ teaspoon baking powder

Angela Says

✱ For the gluten-free flour, I recommend Nu Life Always Gluten Free All-Purpose Flour (304 g) or King Arthur Gluten Free Measure for Measure Flour (270 g).

✱ Don't want cut-out cookies? Roll this dough into a log, wrap with plastic wrap, and freeze for 1 hour. Then remove the dough and slice the dough into ½-inch-thick cookies and bake as above.

✱ You can reroll the scraps from rolling and cutting out these cookies multiple times. Especially when you make these gluten-free, there isn't a chance you will overwork the dough. Just be sure not to incorporate too much flour from your work surface. This can cause the dough to get dry.

Preheat your oven to 350°F. Prepare two baking sheets with parchment paper.

Spread the pecans on a separate dry baking sheet and toast in the oven for about 10 minutes, or until they have a nice nutty aroma and are just a little more brown in color than they were originally. Remove from the oven and set aside to cool. Once the pecans are fully cool, put them in the bowl of a food processor and grind until they resemble a rough flour.

Place the ground pecans, flour, your choice of fat, the powdered sugar, vanilla, salt, and baking powder in the bowl of a stand mixer fitted with the paddle attachment and mix on low speed until combined, then turn up to medium speed to mix until fully combined.

Roll out the dough on a floured work surface to about ¼-inch thickness. The ideal cookie cutter for these cookies is 2 to 3 inches in any direction. We make these as people cutouts, but feel free to use a different shape in the specified dimensions. Cut out the cookies and gently transfer to your prepared baking sheets. I recommend using an offset spatula to move these cookies, as they are a little more delicate than the average cut-out cookie. Using the rounded end of a paintbrush, or another small round end, make slight button indentations going down the front of the cookie.

Bake for 12 to 14 minutes, or until the edges are set and the center gives just a little when you press gently.

Remove from the oven and let cool completely on the baking sheet. Lift these cookies carefully when you transfer them for serving or storing.

SNOW ON PLOWED GROUND COOKIES

These cookies were always just flourless chocolate cookies to me, but one of my first employees introduced them to me as snow on plowed ground, which took me a minute to understand. The chocolate cookie dough is rolled in powdered sugar before baking, then as it bakes and expands, the powdered sugar coating cracks and spreads. It winds up looking like a snow-covered field that has just been plowed in a scattered pattern. The name stuck and its connection to the plains, where we live here in Nebraska, provides such a great earthiness and spirit.

These cookies are so delicious that I almost fell completely on the floor the first time I tried them.

YOU
DO YOU
MAKE THIS
☐ vegan
✗ dairy-free
✗ gluten-free
✗ traditional

YIELD
15 to 20 cookies

Angela Says

✳ The cookies can be kept unbaked in the freezer for up to 1 month. Roll them in the powdered sugar before freezing on a baking sheet or in an airtight container. Bake from frozen and add 2 minutes to baking time.

✳ Be sure not to overmix this cookie dough when you are doing the final mix. Fold everything together until it is just combined, but not so long that the mixture starts to set up as the melted chocolate cools. The mixture will firm up a little bit as it sits and as you scoop, so make sure that doesn't happen just when you are folding.

INGREDIENTS

½ cup (57 g) chopped bittersweet chocolate, dairy-free if necessary

3 large egg whites

2¾ cups (330 g) powdered sugar

¾ cup (67 g) unsweetened cocoa powder

1 teaspoon cornstarch, potato starch, or tapioca starch

1 teaspoon sea salt

Preheat your oven to 350°F and line two baking sheets with parchment paper.

Gently melt the chocolate, either in a saucepan over low heat, or in the microwave. Stir often to make sure the chocolate doesn't overheat or burn in any one area. Set aside to cool while you make the rest of the cookie batter.

Place the egg whites in the bowl of a stand mixer fitted with the whisk attachment and mix on medium speed. Once the whites start to get foamy, sprinkle in 1¼ cups (150 g) of the powdered sugar in small additions, continuing to whisk the egg whites until soft peaks form. Gently fold in the cocoa powder, cornstarch, and salt. Once these additions are mostly folded in (you will still be able to see some streaks of them), add the melted chocolate and fold the rest of the way.

Place the remaining 1½ cups (180 g) of powdered sugar in a small bowl. We use the #24 scoop for our cookies, about 2¾ tablespoons (see page 41). You can also scoop the dough with a large soup spoon. Roll the cookies in the powdered sugar.

Place the cookies about 2 inches apart on the prepared baking sheets. Bake for about 12 minutes, or until the edges of the cookies are set and the middle of the cookie is still soft to the touch.

Remove from the oven and let cool completely on the baking sheets before gently transferring to a storage container or serving tray.

SUGAR COOKIE CUTOUTS

This is an actual foolproof sugar cookie recipe. I have tried it time and time again, in every combination you can imagine: traditional with gluten and dairy, then with dairy and without gluten, without dairy but with gluten, vegan and gluten-free, vegan with gluten. And I have to say, I didn't find a bad option. This sugar cookie doesn't spread when you bake it. It's a traditional "cut-out" recipe—flaky like a shortbread, but sturdy enough to stand up to buttercream and sprinkles. We add almond extract for the classic sugar cookie flavor, but that part can be up to you!

YIELD

20 to 24 cookies, depending on size

Angela Says

✳ For the gluten-free flour, I recommend Bob's Red Mill Gluten Free 1 to 1 Baking Flour (888 g) or King Arthur Gluten Free Measure for Measure Flour (720 g).

✳ If you need the edges to be more refined for an elaborate shape, freeze the cutouts for about 30 minutes before baking. This prevents the cookie from spreading in the oven. For simpler shapes like a circle, you can bake the cookies right away without chilling first.

✳ This dough should be really smooth and easy to roll. If it looks a little dry and is hard to manipulate as you start to roll it out, add a tablespoon of milk at a time and incorporate. The dough should be really soft, but not sticky.

INGREDIENTS

14 ounces (3½ sticks, 309 g) unsalted butter or 1¾ cups (336 g) vegetable shortening

1¾ cups (350 g) granulated sugar

2 large eggs or flax eggs (page 30)

2 teaspoons pure vanilla extract

1 teaspoon almond extract (optional)

2 teaspoons baking powder

1 teaspoon sea salt

6 cups (750 g) all-purpose flour or 6 cups gluten-free all-purpose flour, plus appropriate flour for dusting

2 tablespoons milk, almond milk, or your favorite nondairy milk

1 recipe Classic Vanilla Buttercream (page 223; optional)

Powdered sugar for dusting (optional)

Preheat your oven to 375°F and line two baking sheets with parchment paper.

Combine your choice of fat, sugar, vanilla, and almond extract in the bowl of a stand mixer fitted with the paddle attachment and mix on medium-high speed for about 5 minutes, adding one egg at a time. The mixture should be homogeneous and fluffy. Add the baking powder, salt, and flour and mix on low speed to incorporate. Add the milk and mix to combine. It's important to make sure the cookie dough is well mixed, so be sure to stir it again once you have taken the bowl away from the stand mixer. Fold from the bottom of the bowl to the top, getting everything evenly mixed.

Roll out the dough on a floured work surface to about ¼-inch thickness. The ideal cookie cutter for these cookies is 3 to 4 inches in any direction. Cut out the cookies and gently transfer to your prepared baking sheets. Bake for 12 to 14 minutes, until the edges of the cookies are set and the center feels soft to the touch.

Remove from the oven and let cool completely on the baking sheets or transfer carefully to cooling racks.

These are great without frosting, but you can decorate them with Classic Vanilla Buttercream, or just dust with a little powdered sugar. These keep well at room temperature, in an airtight container, for up to a week. They can be kept frozen for up to 3 weeks.

GINGERBREAD COOKIE CUTOUTS

While everyone else is nibbling on sugar cookies around the holidays, I go straight for spicy gingerbread. For cut-out cookies, it's important that the dough is sturdy enough that the cookies won't spread in the oven. We developed that with this recipe. You can be sure that whatever cookie cutter you use, the shape goes into the oven looking cute, and comes out looking just as great. I make these with and without decoration, but I like them straight off the cookie sheet!

YIELD

30 to 35 cookies, depending on size

INGREDIENTS

10 ounces (2½ sticks, 315 g) unsalted butter or 1¼ cups (240 g) vegetable shortening

1½ cups (269 g) light brown sugar

1 cup (294 g) molasses

1 teaspoon pure vanilla extract

2 large eggs or flax eggs (page 30)

½ teaspoon baking soda

1 teaspoon ground cinnamon

1 teaspoon ground cardamom

2 teaspoons ground ginger

½ teaspoon sea salt

4½ cups (562 g) all-purpose flour or 4½ cups gluten-free all-purpose flour, plus appropriate flour for dusting

1 recipe Classic Vanilla Buttercream (page 223; optional)

Powdered sugar for dusting (optional)

Preheat your oven to 375°F and line two baking sheets with parchment paper.

Combine your choice of fat, brown sugar, molasses, and vanilla in the bowl of a stand mixer fitted with the paddle attachment and mix on medium-high speed for about 5 minutes, adding one egg at a time. The mixture should be homogeneous and fluffy. Add the baking soda, cinnamon, cardamom, ginger, salt, and flour and mix on low speed to incorporate. It's important to make sure the cookie dough is well mixed, so be sure to stir it again once you have taken the bowl away from the stand mixer. Fold from the bottom of the bowl to the top, getting everything evenly mixed.

Roll out the dough on a floured work surface to about ¼-inch thickness. The ideal cookie cutter for these cookies is 3 to 4 inches in any direction. Cut out the cookies and gently transfer to your prepared baking sheets. Bake for 12 to 14 minutes, until the edges of the cookies are set and the center feels soft to the touch.

Remove from the oven and let cool completely on the baking sheets.

Decorate with Classic Vanilla Buttercream, or just dust with a little powdered sugar. These keep well at room temperature, in an airtight container, for up to a week.

Angela Says

✳ For the gluten-free flour, I recommend Nu Life Always Gluten Free All-Purpose Flour (607 g) or King Arthur Gluten Free Measure for Measure Flour (540 g).

PERSIAN LOVE DROPS

These beautiful cookies were inspired by my dear friend Ramin. Originally from Iran, he came to study in Lincoln and we became good friends. He introduced me to the incredible combination of rose and cardamom in cookies, along with the brightness of lemon zest. This is a great winter and holiday cookie, somewhat reminiscent of a shortbread cookie my mom would make, completely rolled in powdered sugar so they would just melt in your mouth.

Recently though, I've been enjoying these year-round. They are sweet little cookies with wonderful flavor and a really beautiful finish, and they don't require much time or decorating patience to look perfect—just what we love.

YIELD

20 to 24 cookies

COOKIE

¼ cup (50 g) granulated sugar

½ cup (60 g) powdered sugar

1 teaspoon ground cardamom

½ teaspoon baking powder

½ teaspoon sea salt

Zest of 1 lemon

2½ cups (313 g) all-purpose flour or 2½ cups gluten-free all-purpose flour

16 tablespoons (2 sticks, 225 g) unsalted butter or 1 cup (192 g) vegetable shortening

GLAZE

2½ cups (300 g) powdered sugar

3 tablespoons milk, almond milk, or your favorite nondairy milk

1 tablespoon rose water

1 dot of pink food coloring

Prepare the cookies: Preheat your oven to 325°F and line two baking sheets with parchment paper.

Combine all the cookie ingredients in the bowl of a stand mixer fitted with the paddle attachment and mix on low speed until the dough comes together to make a loose ball.

Scoop into 1-tablespoon rounds. Place the cookies about 2 inches apart on the prepared baking sheets. Bake for 18 to 20 minutes, or until the edges of the cookies are set and the center doesn't feel soft to the touch at all. They will be a little brown around the bottom edges.

Remove from the oven and let cool completely on the baking sheets or transfer carefully to cooling racks.

While the cookies cool, prepare the glaze: Mix together the powdered sugar, milk, rose water, and food coloring together in a small bowl, using a whisk. Using a spoon, scoop a small amount of glaze on the top of each cooled cookie. We top these with edible glitter, sprinkles, or freeze-dried berry dust for a little extra something special. These will keep really well at room temperature, in an airtight container, for about a week.

Angela Says

✳ For the gluten-free flour, I recommend a mixture of 50% Bob's Red Mill Gluten Free 1 to 1 Baking Flour (185 g) and 50% Nu Life Always Gluten Free All-Purpose Flour (169 g) or a mixture of 50% King Arthur Gluten Free Measure for Measure Flour (150 g) and 50% Bob's Red Mill Gluten Free 1 to 1 Baking Flour (185 g).

SNACK CAKES

Definition of a snack cake: *a cake that is not too sweet, goes well with coffee or tea, and can reasonably be eaten with breakfast, lunch, dinner, and any in-between time that needs a lift. Can also be used as personal motivation to break up the monotony of your day. Snack cakes empower you to take time to eat cake and care for yourself. Must travel well.*

I started thinking about and making snack cakes in 2011, when I was working as a writer in a local biotechnology company. Sitting in a cubicle for eight hours a day didn't get my creative juices flowing, so I relied on little pick-me-ups. These were cakes that I used as motivation during my days. These were cakes I could pack in reusable containers without ruining decoration or design, so it couldn't be anything layered or too elegant. I was obsessed with the concept of meal-prepping for the week, just so I could include my little slices of cake.

Snack cakes make me feel empowered to prepare treats for myself, to make myself food that I know satisfies a deep part of me and makes me unbelievably happy. No guilt. Tearing off pieces of a cake, knowing that I made it for myself, is a very satisfying feeling.

In more specific terms, these are all one layer and include more dessert-type cakes, like the Poppy Seed Bundt Cake (page 114), and more breakfast-type cakes, such as the Extra Special Banana Bread (page 132). All of these cakes will last for three to five days at room temperature. And circling back to the kitchen counter to take off just one more small sliver of cake as you walk by that tempting plate of Spiced Soft Gingerbread Cake (page 138).

LEMON + ALMOND TORTE

One thing I've really loved to experience at Goldenrod is how many kids have come in and made a huge impact on what we do, what we make, and how we keep moving forward. Maya was one such kid. She was about 11 years old when Goldenrod opened, and as a person with celiac disease *and* a sweet tooth, she quickly became a regular. Her mom gifted her with a macaron-making lesson for Christmas one year—I think the first year we opened. We got to spend a few hours with her on a Saturday, making macs, and she was a total natural.

The first time we had this torte in the pastry case, Maya and her mom spotted it on social media. They came in for a slice right away, then came back the next day for even more slices to carry them through the weekend.

This is for Maya.

YOU
DO **YOU**

MAKE THIS

⊔ vegan

✗ dairy-free

✗ gluten-free

✗ traditional

YIELD

One 9-inch round torte

Angela Says

✳ You can change up the flavors in this torte. I think it's great without the addition of lemon zest or the lemon syrup, as a very basic and very delicious almond torte.

✳ This torte has a really delicate rise, which is why it's baked at a lower temperature. We want it to all rise at the same rate, and a lower temperature helps with that. Cranking up the oven temperature can mean the outside ring of the torte is done before the center, and you can risk the center of the torte rising too fast and then falling.

TORTE

Nonstick spray for pan

½ pound (2 sticks, 225 g) unsalted butter, at room temperature, or 1 cup (192 g) vegetable shortening

1 cup (200 g) granulated sugar

3 large eggs

2¾ cups (264 g) almond flour

1½ teaspoons baking powder

Zest of 2 lemons (save the juice!)

GLAZE

Juice of 2 lemons

¾ cup (90 g) powdered sugar

Prepare the torte: Preheat your oven to 325°F. Spray a 9-inch round cake pan with nonstick spray and line it with parchment paper.

Place your choice of fat, granulated sugar, and eggs in the bowl of a stand mixer fitted with the paddle attachment and mix until all is combined and fluffy, 3 to 5 minutes, stopping the mixer to scrape the sides of the bowl as needed. You'll know this mixture is ready when it is a pale yellow color and has some added volume. Add the almond flour, baking powder, and lemon zest. Mix to combine.

Pour into your prepared cake pan and bake for about 35 minutes, or until golden brown and a paring knife inserted into the center comes out clean. Remove from the oven and set aside to cool in the pan.

Once the cake is cool, run a knife around the edge of the cake, maintaining contact with the pan the entire time. Turn the cake out onto a piece of parchment paper or a plate, then place another plate on top to flip the cake back over to be right-side up.

Prepare the glaze: Combine the lemon juice and powdered sugar in a small saucepan and heat over medium heat until the sugar dissolves. Pour over the torte while it is still hot in the pan. This amount of glaze will really soak the cake. Use less if you want a drier cake.

Serve just like this, or with a little dollop of Goldenrod's Favorite Lemon Curd (page 236).

APPLE SNACK CAKE

I remember bringing this cake to a Hanukkah dinner. I'm known for making way too much food for the number of people who will be eating, and this occasion was no different. We were with our friends Steve and Amy, and their daughter, Poppy. The meal was dynamite, and we were stuffed to the point of pain. So, when I brought out this apple cake, we all groaned and said, "Maybe just, like, a sliver." Okay, so a sliver here and a sliver there ended up with most of the cake gone between four adults and one six-year-old.

The apples are barely held together by the batter. It's just as good, if not better, for the next few days as it is the day you make it. I make this recipe with Granny Smith apples, because they are super tart and hold together really well through baking.

YOU
DO **YOU**

MAKE THIS

☐ vegan

✗ dairy-free

✗ gluten-free

✗ traditional

YIELD

One 9-inch round cake

INGREDIENTS

Nonstick spray for pan

4 Granny Smith or other tart apples

1 tablespoon ground cardamom

1 cup (200 g) plus 2 tablespoons (25 g) granulated sugar

½ cup (120 ml) melted coconut oil or vegetable oil

¼ cup (60 ml) fresh lemon juice

1 teaspoon pure vanilla extract

2 large eggs

1⅓ cups (167 g) all-purpose flour or 1⅓ cups gluten-free all-purpose flour

½ teaspoon baking powder

½ teaspoon sea salt

½ cup (60 g) walnut pieces (optional)

Powdered sugar for dusting

Preheat your oven to 350°F. Grease a 9-inch cake pan with nonstick spray and line it with parchment paper.

Core the apples and chop into 1-inch pieces. I don't find it necessary to peel them, but if you don't want peel in your cake, feel free to peel the apples! Toss them into a medium bowl with the cardamom and 2 tablespoons of granulated sugar. Set aside while you make the batter.

Combine the oil, granulated sugar, lemon juice, vanilla, and eggs in a large bowl. Whisk well, then add the flour, baking powder, and salt. Mix together with a spoon, then fold in the apples and walnuts.

Pour into your prepared pan and bake for 40 minutes, or until the edges have pulled away from the side of the cake (always a good indicator that your cake is done!). Remove from the oven and let the cake cool in the pan for about 30 minutes before you unmold it.

This is great on the first day because the edges are still crispy, but it is also so good for the next few days. Dust with powdered sugar to serve—it will look so fancy.

Angela Says

✳ For the gluten-free flour, I recommend Bob's Red Mill Gluten Free 1 to 1 Baking Flour (197 g).

POPPY SEED BUNDT CAKE

I wanted to make a cake that reminds me of the months I spent in Poland while I was in college. I never figured out how to use public transportation, so I ended up walking two or three miles to school every day. This walk took me past a big food hall with a pastry stall right at the entrance where I'd buy a sweet roll with a poppy seed filling. No glaze, no sugar on the outside, just the sweetness from the dough and the deep nutty sweetness from the filling.

I grew up thinking that poppy seeds had to be accompanied by lemon, orange, or almond. But this is an unadulterated poppy seed cake—no lemon, orange, or almond. If you haven't tried a pastry with just poppy seeds, I really recommend trying this cake. These pastries are found often in Eastern Europe. You get so much nuttiness from just a whole bunch of poppy seeds.

YOU
DO YOU

MAKE THIS

⊐ vegan
✗ dairy-free
✗ gluten-free
✗ traditional

YIELD

One 10-inch round cake

INGREDIENTS

Nonstick spray for pan, plus granulated sugar for dusting

1½ cups (360 ml) milk, almond milk, or your favorite nondairy milk

1¼ cups (300 ml) vegetable oil

3 large eggs

3 cups (375 g) all-purpose flour or 3 cups gluten-free all-purpose flour

2½ cups (500 g) granulated sugar

1½ tablespoons baking powder

1 teaspoon sea salt

½ cup (68 g) poppy seeds

1 recipe Classic Vanilla Glaze (page 221)

Preheat your oven to 400°F and spray a 12-cup fluted cake pan or Bundt pan with nonstick spray and dust with granulated sugar (we do this to help the cake unmold from the pan, and to give a great little crust on the outside).

This cake couldn't be any simpler. Put all the ingredients in the bowl of a stand mixer fitted with the paddle attachment and mix on medium-high speed for 5 minutes.

Pour into your prepared pan and bake for about 55 minutes. It's done when it pulls away from the edges, is a nice golden brown all over, and the tallest part of the cake barely gives when you poke it. While the cake bakes, prepare your Classic Vanilla Glaze.

Remove from the oven and let cool for about 5 minutes in the pan, before gently unmolding it and allowing it to cool at room temperature.

Drizzle the Classic Vanilla Glaze over the cake and serve.

Angela Says

✳ For the gluten-free flour, I recommend Bob's Red Mill Gluten Free 1 to 1 Baking Flour (444 g).

MARZIPAN CAKE
WITH STRAWBERRIES

I used to have such a hard time buying bulk marzipan for myself when I baked at home, and then at the bakery. I somehow never had it around when I wanted or needed it—and because Lincoln isn't a town in Scandinavia, nor does it have a large Scandinavian population, it really was hard to find. Until one day, it dawned on me that I could just make marzipan myself, which felt like a revelation. A revelation that, as a professional pastry chef, I should have had much sooner! Good news is, it's so easy to make, you can have it on hand at a moment's notice.

This cake uses marzipan as part of the fat, and it is great and light and moist—and nice and rich from the marzipan. You can make the cake as I did here with strawberries, you can use a different fruit like peaches or apricots—or you can just make this cake on its own. It's totally lovely as is.

YIELD

One 13-by-18-inch cake

MARZIPAN

1 cup (120 g) powdered sugar

1¼ cups (120 g) blanched almond flour

1 large egg white

½ teaspoon sea salt

1 teaspoon almond extract

Angela Says

✱ For the gluten-free flour, I recommend Bob's Red Mill Gluten Free 1 to 1 Baking Flour (407 g).

✱ You can also make these as mini cupcakes! See the photo on pages 118–119.

✱ You can substitute 1½ cups store-bought almond paste if you don't want to make marzipan from scratch.

CAKE

Nonstick spray for pan

1 cup (240 ml) milk, almond milk, or your favorite nondairy milk

2 teaspoons white distilled or cider vinegar

½ pound (2 sticks, 225 g) unsalted butter or 1 cup (192 g) vegetable shortening

1 cup (200 g) granulated sugar

2¾ cups (344 g) all-purpose flour or 2¾ cups gluten-free all-purpose flour

1 teaspoon sea salt

1 teaspoon pure vanilla extract

1 cup (about 150 g) hulled and halved strawberries (or peaches, apricots, or cherries—whatever you love)

½ cup (80 g) sliced almonds

Make the marzipan: Put all the marzipan ingredients in a food processor and process on high speed until the mixture is all smooth and evenly combined, 1 to 2 minutes. You can store it at room temperature if you're going to use it the same day; otherwise, I recommend keeping it in the fridge. Take it out of the fridge before you use it to bring it to room temperature.

Make the cake: Preheat your oven to 350°F and spray a 13-by-18-inch baking pan with nonstick spray. The great thing about this cake is that you can bake it in just about any shape. You can cut it into squares, but it works well in little tea cake pans, as cupcakes, in a loaf pan, or even a Bundt pan. Use what you have on hand and works for your occasion. It'll make a couple dozen cupcakes, two large loaves, or one Bundt cake.

Combine the milk and vinegar in a cup or small bowl, mix together with a fork, and set aside.

Cream together the marzipan, your choice of fat, and the granulated sugar in the bowl of a stand mixer fitted with the paddle attachment. Add the eggs and mix until homogeneous, scraping down the sides of the bowl as needed. Add the flour, salt, and vanilla. Start the mixer on low speed and slowly stream in the milk mixture. Scrape down the sides of the bowl and give it a good mix on high speed to make sure everything is well incorporated.

Pour your batter into your prepared pan and sprinkle with the fruit. Sprinkle with the sliced almonds. Bake for about 30 minutes in a 13-by-18-inch pan, or for 18 minutes in smaller, individual pans. The cake is fully baked when it is a nice golden brown, the edges of the cake are coming away from the edge of the pan, and the center of the cake barely gives when you gently poke it.

CHOCOLATE THUNDER CAKE

ADAPTED FROM THE RECIPE IN *THUNDER CAKE* BY PATRICIA POLACCO

Although I don't remember being scared of thunder and lightning as a child, I do vividly recall my mother and grandmother reading the book *Thunder Cake* to me. In it, a nervous little girl is being comforted by her grandmother—whom she calls Babushka—by baking a cake together. They have to gather all the ingredients for "thunder cake" before the rain starts. They go to the chicken coop and grab eggs, to the barn to get milk, and even to the garden for a few tomatoes. They get back to the house, make the cake, and put it in the oven just as the rain starts.

The grandma in the story is very no-nonsense, with the idea to focus on a project rather than on fear. I think I internalized this message and have carried it with me ever since.

This cake is an homage to the one in the story—the tomato puree adds extra moisture to an already lovely chocolate cake. Even in the best of weather, this is a great cake to take when you're on the move, when you need a slice of something at 2 p.m., or to have with berries and ice cream as a dessert.

YOU
DO YOU

MAKE THIS

⊐ vegan

✗ dairy-free

✗ gluten-free

✗ traditional

YIELD

Two 9-by-5-inch loaves

INGREDIENTS

Nonstick spray for pan

½ pound (2 sticks, 225 g) unsalted butter or 1 cup (192 g) vegetable shortening

1¾ cups (350 g) granulated sugar

3 large eggs

1 teaspoon sea salt

1 teaspoon pure vanilla extract

2½ cups (313 g) all-purpose flour or 2½ cups gluten-free all-purpose flour

½ cup (45 g) unsweetened cocoa powder

1½ teaspoons baking soda

1 cup (240 ml) water

½ cup (120 ml) fresh or canned tomato puree

Chocolate Oven Ganache (page 232; optional)

Angela Says

✳ For the gluten-free flour, I recommend Bob's Red Mill Gluten Free 1 to 1 Baking Flour (370 g).

✳ The addition of tomato puree adds a little sweetness, moisture, and a bit of acid.

Preheat your oven to 350°F and grease two 9-by-5-inch loaf pans with nonstick spray. I like to line my pan with parchment paper as well, but this cake unmolds well without the paper if you don't have it.

Combine your choice of fat and the sugar in the bowl of a stand mixer fitted with a paddle attachment and cream together for about a minute, or until light and fluffy. Add the eggs, salt, and vanilla and cream again to incorporate. Add the flour, cocoa powder, and baking soda. Start your mixer on low and stream in the water and tomato puree. Your batter will be nice and fluffy—make sure to scrape down the sides of the bowl as needed to ensure the batter is homogenous.

Pour your luscious batter into the prepared loaf pans. Bake this cake for about 45 minutes, or until the edges start to come away from the pan, a knife inserted into the center of a loaf comes out clean, and the cake barely gives when you poke it gently with your finger.

Remove from the oven and let cool in the pans for 5 to 10 minutes, then remove from the pans to cool at room temperature the rest of the way. You can let them cool on your counter or a cooling rack.

Top with Chocolate Oven Ganache for an extra-special treat. Slather it on and keep some on the side if you feel like dipping.

ZUCCHINI CHOCOLATE CAKE

My mom makes the best zucchini chocolate cake. It is so easy to keep taking thin slices from the pan with a butter knife. You just think that if you walk by the pan that's sitting on the counter and take a morsel, no one will even notice. Eventually, after you walk by for the 14th time, someone is going to notice that a third of the pan disappeared in 20 minutes. I think my favorite part of this recipe is that about halfway through the baking time, she sprinkles chocolate chips and granulated sugar over the top. They both melt into the top of the cake, but don't bake so long that they overbake and get burned or too crunchy.

This is the Goldenrod version of her recipe.

We worked up this recipe during the first summer the shop was open. I really wanted to focus on using local ingredients and produce when I opened Goldenrod, but that was proving kind of hard to do with pastries unless I wanted to do more savory options. So, we started looking for ways to use what was already there, and to make some childhood favorites in our new, inclusive way of baking. This is a customer favorite that we are thrilled to bring back every summer.

We've tried baking this cake in just about every shape and size, and it's great any way you bake it.

YOU DO YOU
MAKE THIS
- ❏ vegan
- ✗ dairy-free
- ✗ gluten-free
- ✗ traditional

YIELD
One 9-by-13-inch cake

INGREDIENTS

Nonstick spray for pan

4 large eggs

1 cup (200 g) granulated sugar, plus more for dusting and 2 tablespoons for sprinkling

1 cup (179 g) light brown sugar

1 cup (240 ml) vegetable oil or melted coconut oil

½ teaspoon sea salt

½ teaspoon baking soda

1½ teaspoons baking powder

¾ cup (67 g) cocoa powder

2 cups (250 g) all-purpose flour or 2 cups gluten-free all-purpose flour

3 cups (360 g) grated zucchini

½ cup (77 g) bittersweet chocolate chips, dairy-free if necessary

Preheat your oven to 375°F. Grease a 9-by-13-inch baking pan with nonstick spray and dust it with granulated sugar.

Combine the eggs, both sugars, and oil in a large bowl and mix using a wooden spoon. Add the flour, salt, baking powder, baking soda, and cocoa powder and mix again to incorporate, scraping down the sides of the bowl as necessary. If your grated zucchini feels very heavy with moisture, I recommend squeezing out some of the liquid before adding the zucchini. You can do this by putting the grated zucchini in a clean tea towel and wringing it out over a bowl or sink. Add the zucchini and mix to combine.

Pour the batter into your prepared baking pan. Bake for about 10 minutes, then sprinkle the chocolate chips and 2 tablespoons of granulated sugar over the top of the cake and bake for another 20 to 25 minutes, until the edges start to pull away from the side of the pan a little, the center of the cake just barely gives when you gently press it with your finger, and a cake tester or paring knife inserted into the center comes out clean.

This cake is great eaten warm, or at room temperature. You can store this at room temperature, covered, for about 5 days.

Angela Says

✳ For the gluten-free flour, I recommend Bob's Red Mill Gluten Free 1 to 1 Baking Flour (296 g).

✳ Bake this in lined muffin tins for a rich and delicious breakfast treat.

FUNERAL BROWNIES

This is a beloved family favorite that I adapted from a Nigella Lawson recipe. They are the best combination of fudgy brownie texture with a little bit of a cakey texture as well. I serve these as a full-on dessert, perfect to eat with friends at a dinner party, and are absolutely fancy enough for any occasion.

We started calling these Funeral Brownies in my house when I made them to eat after my Grandma Cariotto's funeral in 2006. I think I made a few hundred of them. We all flocked to the tray of stacked brownies for comfort. And they became the go-to for when the hardest days need the sweetest treats.

But definitely do not save these for just the hard days—I can verify they are great to be eaten all the time.

YIELD

One 9-by-13-inch pan

INGREDIENTS

Nonstick spray for pan

1²/₃ cups (400 ml) melted coconut oil

13 ounces (369 g) bittersweet chocolate, chopped, or chips, dairy-free if necessary

1²/₃ cups (333 g) granulated sugar

6 large eggs

2 teaspoons pure vanilla extract

1 teaspoon sea salt

1½ cups (188 g) all-purpose flour or 1½ cups gluten-free all-purpose flour

1²/₃ cups (208 g) walnut pieces (optional)

Angela Says

✳ For the gluten-free flour, I recommend Bob's Red Mill Gluten Free 1 to 1 Baking Flour (222 g) or King Arthur Flour Gluten Free Measure for Measure (180 g).

✳ Take these brownies out of the oven when the edges are set and the center of the pan is matte and starting to crack a little. These are the cues that your brownies are perfectly baked!

Preheat your oven to 325°F. Spray a 9-by-13-inch baking pan with nonstick spray and line with parchment paper. I like to make sure the parchment paper extends over the sides of the pan so I can lift out the brownies easily.

Gently melt together the coconut oil and chocolate. You can do this over low heat on the stove, or in the microwave, stirring often to prevent burning. Set aside to cool.

While the melted chocolate mixture is cooling, whisk together the sugar, eggs, and vanilla in a large bowl. Once well mixed, add the cooled chocolate mixture and whisk to combine. Add the salt, flour, and walnuts (if using). Fold everything together with a spatula until there aren't any spots of raw flour left in the mixture. The batter will be very shiny and thick.

Pour the brownie batter into the prepared pan and make sure to spread it out evenly. Bake for 40 to 50 minutes, or until the edges are firm to the touch, and the center just barely gives when you gently press it with your finger, and when a knife or toothpick inserted into the center comes out with a little chocolate still on the end. You want the brownies a little gooey in the center!

Remove from the oven and let cool completely in the pan, then gently pull the edges of parchment paper up to release the brownies from the pan. Cut into small pieces to serve—they are very rich!

FROSTED BROWNIES

If you are a fudgy-brownie lover, I am happy to refer you to my recipe for Funeral Brownies (page 124). And if you are a cake-brownie lover, welcome home. We're happy to have you here! This recipe is for you. This is the kind of brownie your teeth just sink right into. I love them with or without frosting, but frosting is a great addition. I, personally, am an "edge person," meaning I am the one trying to grab a corner brownie piece before anyone else can get to it. And I can attest to these brownies having excellent corners.

Their center pieces are great, too. These are so festive with frosting and sprinkles.

YOU DO YOU

MAKE THIS

✗ vegan

✗ dairy-free

✗ gluten-free

✗ traditional

YIELD
One 13-by-18-inch pan

INGREDIENTS

Nonstick spray for pan

4 cups (500 g) all-purpose flour or 4 cups gluten-free all-purpose flour

3 cups (600 g) granulated sugar

¾ cup (68 g) unsweetened cocoa powder

1½ teaspoons baking powder

1½ teaspoons sea salt

1½ cups (360 ml) water

1½ cups (360 ml) vegetable oil

1 recipe Dark Chocolate Buttercream (page 225)

Angela Says

✳ For the gluten-free flour, I recommend Bob's Red Mill Gluten Free 1 to 1 Baking Flour (592 g).

Preheat your oven to 350°F and spray a 13-by-18-inch rimmed baking sheet with nonstick spray.

Combine the flour, sugar, cocoa, baking powder, salt, and water in the bowl of a stand mixer fitted with the paddle attachment. Start the mixer on the lowest speed to start incorporating everything, and start slowly streaming in the oil. Once all the oil is added and the mixture has come together, increase the mixer speed to medium and let mix for about 3 minutes. The mixture will change significantly from being a somewhat craggly batter to having a very smooth and almost ribbonlike consistency.

Once smooth and ribbonlike, pour the batter into your prepared pan. Spread evenly across the pan, making sure to get batter to the edges and in the corners. Bake for about 20 minutes, or until the edges of the brownies are firm to the touch and the center just barely gives when you gently press it with your finger. The top of the brownie will have a matte finish when they are done.

Remove from the oven and let cool completely in the pan. Once cooled, top with Dark Chocolate Buttercream. At Goldenrod, we make frosting swoops across the top, but finish these how you like! Add your favorite sprinkles, or leave as is!

These store great at room temperature, covered, for up to 4 days.

PEACH + BUCKWHEAT

UPSIDE-DOWN CAKE

Traditional upside-down cakes have always appealed to me because of the idea of flipping over a cake to reveal a surprise underneath. This particular upside-down cake is not too sweet and I can eat it for breakfast dessert, lunch dessert, during the afternoon with tea, or with Whipped Coconut Cream (page 230) as a fancier dessert. This is the ideal snack cake.

Here, the bright, sweet summer peaches contrast perfectly with the earthiness of buckwheat. It's a great combination that I am pretty passionate about!

Make this cake in the winter by replacing the peaches with pears. I use Bosc, Anjou, or Bartlett pears for baking. You'll prepare the cake exactly the same way as the recipe states—just substitute pears for the peaches.

YOU
DO YOU
MAKE THIS
✗ vegan
✗ dairy-free
✗ gluten-free
✗ traditional

YIELD
One 9-inch round cake

Angela Says

✳ For the gluten-free flour, I recommend Bob's Red Mill Gluten Free 1 to 1 Baking Flour (296 g).

✳ If you are feeling a little less ambitious and don't want to layer fruit to be upside down, simply chop the fruit and mix it into the batter. Omit the caramel and brown sugar.

✳ If you don't have any fruit around, this cake is great without! Just omit the caramel, pour the cake batter directly into the prepared pan, and sprinkle the brown sugar on top before the cake goes in the oven.

INGREDIENTS

Nonstick spray for pan

2 cups (250 g) all-purpose flour or 2 cups gluten-free all-purpose flour

1 cup (143 g) buckwheat flour

2 teaspoons baking powder

1⅓ cups (267 g) granulated sugar

Zest of 1 lemon

¾ cup (180 ml) olive oil

2 cups (480 ml) milk, almond milk, or your favorite nondairy milk

2 teaspoons pure vanilla extract

4 peaches, unpeeled

¼ cup (44 g) light brown sugar

½ cup (120 ml) Caramel Sauce (page 234)

Preheat your oven to 375°F. Spray a 9-inch round cake pan with nonstick spray and line with parchment paper.

Whisk together the flour, buckwheat flour, baking powder, sugar, and lemon zest in a medium bowl. Add the oil, milk, and vanilla and mix to combine completely.

Slice the peaches in half and split open to release the pit. Then, slice into ½-inch-wide half-moons. Sprinkle the brown sugar on the bottom of the prepared cake pan, add the caramel, then arrange the peaches in a nice wheel pattern. Gently pour the batter over the arranged peaches and spread in an even layer.

Bake for about 35 minutes, or until the cake is pulling away from the sides of the pan and a paring knife or cake tester inserted into the center comes out clean.

Remove from the oven and let the cake cool in the pan for about 5 minutes before carefully unmolding onto a plate. It's okay if the peaches move around a little bit when you are unmolding—just put them back in place.

BEST POUND CAKE

When I stopped eating dairy, I resigned myself to not eating some of my very favorite treats. Pound cake was one of them. I was pleasantly surprised to find that vegetable shortening, especially when I used almond extract and both orange and lemon zests, made an equally-compelling loaf. This is the kind of cake you want to keep a loaf of in your freezer at all times, just in case (a) you have a craving, or (b) you have unexpected guests. For me, it's usually because I just need cake. I could suggest that you eat it with macerated berries, lemon curd, homemade preserves . . .

But it really doesn't need anything.

This is the kind of cake you find in French bakeries. It has a slight almond essence, an incredibly delicate crumb on the outside, and a very tender, moist, and perfectly dense interior. If you do choose to make this gluten-free, it's even better than with gluten. It's great either way, but the lack of gluten in the batter means it stays really tender. (Read more on this in the Ingredients section, page 32.)

YOU DO YOU
MAKE THIS
- ⊔ vegan
- ✗ dairy-free
- ✗ gluten-free
- ✗ traditional

YIELD
One 9-by-5-inch loaf

INGREDIENTS

Nonstick spray for pan

16 tablespoons (2 sticks, 225 g) unsalted butter, at room temperature, or 1 cup (192 g) vegetable shortening

1½ cups (300 g) granulated sugar

Zest of 1 orange

Zest of 1 lemon

5 large eggs

1 teaspoon almond or pure vanilla extract

2 teaspoons baking powder

2 cups (250 g) all-purpose flour or 2 cups gluten-free all-purpose flour

Preheat your oven to 350°F. Spray a 9-by-5-inch loaf pan with nonstick spray and line with parchment paper.

Combine your choice of fat, sugar, and citrus zests in the bowl of a stand mixer fitted with the paddle attachment. Beat on medium speed until everything is fluffy and totally homogeneous. Add the eggs, one at a time, and beat to incorporate completely after each addition. Once all the eggs are added and the mixture is fully mixed, add the extract, baking powder, and flour. Mix just to combine, scraping the sides of the bowl and mixing again to make sure everything is mixed well.

Pour the batter evenly into the prepared pan. Bake for 50 to 60 minutes, until the edges pull away from the sides of the pan, the cake is a nice golden brown all over, and the center barely gives when you poke it.

Remove from the oven and let cool for about 15 minutes in the pan before running a paring knife around the edges and gently unmolding.

Angela Says

✳ For the gluten-free flour, I recommend Bob's Red Mill Gluten Free 1 to 1 Baking Flour (296 g).

EXTRA SPECIAL BANANA BREAD

This is one of the all-time favorite, always-on-the-menu Goldenrod standards: the perfect banana bread. The loaf is rich and moist, with a pronounced crust on all four edges, and incredible texture from the seeds, nuts, and sugar sprinkled on the top of the loaf. I love that when you hold one side of the piece, it's tender enough to almost split in half just from gravity pulling it down. By far, my favorite banana bread.

I made this recipe for two loaves because it's so good you might eat an entire loaf while it's still warm, and you'll be thankful you have that second loaf around!

YIELD

Two 9-by-5-inch loaves

BREAD

Nonstick spray for pans

3 ripe, speckled bananas (365 g)

1½ cups (300 g) granulated sugar

3 large eggs

1 cup (240 g) neutral oil (we use vegetable oil)

1 teaspoon pure vanilla extract

¾ teaspoon sea salt

2 teaspoons baking powder

½ teaspoon baking soda

2¼ cups (281 g) all-purpose flour or 2¼ cups gluten-free all-purpose flour

TOPPING

4 teaspoons sesame seeds (we use both white and black seeds, but use what you have)

½ cup (75 g) walnut pieces

2 tablespoons granulated sugar

GLAZE

¾ cup (90 g) powdered sugar

2 tablespoons milk, almond milk, or your favorite nondairy milk

½ teaspoon pure vanilla extract

Preheat your oven to 350°F. Spray two 9-by-5-inch loaf pans with nonstick spray and line with parchment paper.

You can make this recipe with a stand mixer, or with just a bowl and a fork. Like I always say, use what you have. Your first step is to smash together the bananas and sugar. If you're using a stand mixer, use the paddle attachment. Once this is a nice smooshy texture, add the eggs and oil and mix to combine. From there, add the vanilla, salt, baking powder, baking soda, and flour and mix thoroughly to incorporate. Make sure all the lumps of flour have disappeared in the mess of banana goodness.

Divide the batter evenly between the two prepared pans, and start topping! I recommend sprinkling sesame seeds on the cake first, then the walnut pieces, and then the sugar for the final touch. You are sprinkling *just enough* sugar on the top of each loaf—enough to add some crunch but not so much that the loaf is difficult to slice through. This order allows for each ingredient to stick to the batter the best it can.

Bake for about 55 minutes, or until completely golden brown across the entire cake, and the center barely gives back when you poke it. You can unmold as soon as the pan is cool enough to touch.

These store great at room temperature for 3 days, and can be wrapped tightly in plastic wrap and frozen for up to 2 weeks. Glaze after thawing when ready to eat.

Make the glaze: Whisk together the powdered sugar, milk, and vanilla in a small bowl until completely smooth. Drizzle over the top of the finished loaves of banana bread.

Angela Says

* For the gluten-free flour, I recommend Pamela's Gluten-Free All-Purpose Flour (270 g).

PUMPKIN LOAF CAKE

This cake is a great example of a recipe being vegan without any dairy or egg substitutes—it's simply vegan on its own! The pumpkin puree works well as a binder, so you don't need to worry about adding eggs to hold this together. You can bake this loaf cake recipe as a layered birthday cake with cinnamon frosting; in muffin form; and as a great baked donut.

This recipe comes together really quickly—you can have pumpkin cake for you and your friends in no time!

YIELD

Two 9-by-5-inch loaves

INGREDIENTS

Nonstick spray for pans

3½ cups (438 g) all-purpose flour or 3½ cups gluten-free all-purpose flour

2⅔ cups (476 g) light brown sugar

2 teaspoons baking soda

1 teaspoon baking powder

1 teaspoon sea salt

1 teaspoon ground cinnamon

1 teaspoon ground ginger

1 teaspoon ground cardamom

¼ teaspoon freshly ground black pepper

1 cup (240 ml) vegetable oil

⅔ cup (160 ml) water

One 15-ounce (424 g) can pure pumpkin puree

½ cup (60 g) pumpkin seeds

2 tablespoons granulated sugar for sprinkling

Preheat your oven to 375°F. Spray two 9-by-5-inch loaf pans with nonstick spray and line with parchment paper.

Whisk together the flour, brown sugar, baking soda, baking powder, sea salt, cinnamon, ginger, cardamom, and pepper in a large bowl until everything is evenly combined and there are no lumps of sugar or flour. Add the oil and water and whisk again to incorporate. You will probably have to switch over to mixing with a rubber spatula or spoon at this point. Add the pumpkin puree and mix to combine everything completely, making sure to scoop from the bottom of the bowl to get everything well blended.

Divide between the two prepared loaf pans. Arrange half of the pumpkin seeds on top of each loaf and sprinkle half of the granulated sugar on top of each loaf. Bake for 80 to 90 minutes, until the edges of the cake release from the edge side of the pan, the top is golden brown, and the center of the cake barely gives back when you press it gently with your finger. You can also insert a knife into the center of a cake to check doneness—the knife should come out completely clean.

Remove from the oven and let the cakes cool in their pans for about 15 minutes before gently removing and letting them cool at room temperature.

Angela Says

* For the gluten-free flour, I recommend Bob's Red Mill Gluten Free 1 to 1 Baking Flour (518 g).

PUMPKIN CAKE DONUTS

We make these donuts regularly at the bakery during the fall and winter months—and during the rest of the year for special orders when people can't get enough of them! This is a baked donut, the only kind I mess with, to be honest. But to make sure we still get a bit of crunch and that slightly oily feeling we associate with a donut, I dip these in melted coconut oil. It soaks in to the outside of the cake donut and creates almost a bit of a crunch.

I double-dip these into a sugar-and-spice blend that includes a hint of black pepper. The donut is already sweet enough, so I love amping up the flavor in the outside spice mix!

YIELD

12 donuts

INGREDIENTS

Nonstick spray for pan

1 recipe (see directions) Pumpkin Loaf Cake (page 135)

½ cup (120 ml) melted coconut oil

1½ cups (300 g) granulated sugar

¾ teaspoon freshly ground black pepper

1 teaspoon ground cinnamon

1 teaspoon ground cardamom

Preheat your oven to 400°F. Spray two six-donut pans with nonstick spray. (If you have only one pan, bake half of the batter, then respray the pan and bake the remaining batter.)

Make the Pumpkin Loaf Cake batter according to the recipe directions.

Fill a piping bag or resealable plastic freezer bag with some of the pumpkin batter, and cut off the tip of the bag to make a 1-inch opening. Pipe the batter into your prepared donut pans, adding just enough batter to reach the top of each donut mold. Repeat until all the donut molds are full.

Bake for about 15 minutes, or until the donuts are browned on the edges and barely give back when you gently touch the center. You will want to unmold these right away so they don't continue to cook. Over a sheet pan, or directly over your counter, gently tap the edges of the donut pans so the donuts fall out onto the pan or counter.

Pour the melted coconut oil in a small bowl. In a separate bowl, combine the sugar, pepper, cinnamon, and cardamom. Once the donuts are cool, dip them in the coconut oil and place back on their pan or a plate. Once all donuts have been dipped in coconut oil, go back to the first donut and dip in the spiced sugar. Each donut should get two spiced sugar dips for maximum spice!

Enjoy these on the day you make them.

SPICED SOFT GINGERBREAD CAKE

Gingerbread has always been a really elusive and mysterious cake to me. When I was in high school, I discovered a recipe for it in a bargain-bin cookbook and made it immediately. I was inspired by another cookbook to poach pears at the same time, and ate the two deluxe treats together. The dark density of gingerbread cake is one I've never found in another cake. It's so perfect with a crisp beer, or a deep red wine.

I knew I wanted to sell gingerbread in the bakery, because it is such a hard-to-find cake. There were some people who flocked almost immediately to buy a slice because it reminded them of something they'd had before—which is one of the best compliments a chef can receive. Other people quickly found their new favorite cake. The darkness of this cake is best during the fall and winter months, but I'm happy to eat it any time of year.

YIELD
One 9-inch round cake

INGREDIENTS

Nonstick spray for pan

⅓ cup (98 g) molasses

½ cup (80 g) pure maple syrup

½ cup (89 g) light brown sugar

¾ cup (180 g) water

5 tablespoons (75 g) unsalted butter, at room temperature or ⅓ cup (80 ml) vegetable or melted coconut oil

3 large eggs

1 teaspoon ground cinnamon

1 teaspoon ground ginger

1 teaspoon grated fresh ginger (optional)

½ teaspoon sea salt

¾ teaspoon baking soda

2 cups (250 g) all-purpose flour or 2 cups gluten-free all-purpose flour

Classic Vanilla Glaze (page 221; optional)

Angela Says

✳ For the gluten-free flour, I recommend Nu Life Always Gluten Free All-Purpose Flour (270 g) or King Arthur Gluten Free Measure for Measure Flour (240 g).

Preheat your oven to 350°F. You can bake this in a 9-inch round cake pan or a 9-by-5-inch loaf pan. It's a sticky batter, so be sure to spray your pan with nonstick spray and line with parchment paper.

Combine the molasses, maple syrup, brown sugar, and water in a saucepan over medium-low heat. Melt everything together, whisking to make a nice little sugary syrup, about 5 minutes. Pour into a large bowl and set aside to cool for a few minutes.

You can mix this by hand with a whisk or with a stand mixer fitted with the whisk attachment. To the syrup, add the oil, eggs, cinnamon, ground ginger, fresh ginger (if using), and salt. Mix just to combine. Add the baking soda and flour and whisk until incorporated and the batter is homogeneous.

Pour into the prepared pan and bake for about 50 minutes. This cake takes a little while to bake because it is such a liquidy batter. The top of your cake will be a little dark because it takes so long to cook through. You'll know it's done when the edges of the cake pull away from the pan, the top of the cake is a little shiny, and it barely gives back when you poke it with your finger.

Remove from the oven and let cool completely before unmolding from the pan on a cooling rack or plate. Glaze with Classic Vanilla Glaze, or just eat it on its own. This cake is super moist and will keep great at room temperature for a week. Freeze it by the slice if you want to grab it as needed!

HONEY CAKE

I was an avid reader as a child, and seem to have been drawn to stories in which food played a role! In one of my favorites, honey cake was wrapped in a cloth and packed in the young characters' lunches. In the illustrations, the cake looked soft but dense, perfectly golden, and packable. I imagined it was probably sitting on the counter all week, getting packed up little by little every day. I wanted to be those kids, with their little bundle of honey cake, even though my mom totally sent me on the walk to school with a full slice of fresh blueberry pie.

There is a good helping of spice in this cake, but you can easily omit the spices to make just a deep honey-flavored cake. Some honey cakes call for brewed coffee in the batter, but I also use brewed rooibos tea. It feels so earthy and perfect that way to me.

YOU
DO **YOU**

MAKE THIS

⊐ vegan

✗ dairy-free

✗ gluten-free

✗ traditional

YIELD

One 9-by-13-inch cake

INGREDIENTS

Nonstick spray for pan

3½ cups (438 g) all-purpose flour or 3½ cups gluten-free all-purpose flour

1 teaspoon baking powder

1 teaspoon baking soda

½ teaspoon sea salt

2 teaspoons ground cinnamon

1 teaspoon ground cardamom

1 cup (240 ml) vegetable oil or melted coconut oil

1 cup (298 g) honey

1 cup (200 g) granulated sugar

½ cup (89 g) light brown sugar

3 large eggs

1 cup (240 ml) brewed tea (I like rooibos, but black tea would also work)

½ cup (120 ml) fresh lemon juice

½ cup (120 ml) bourbon, or use ½ cup orange juice if you don't want to use alcohol

½ cup (62 g) slivered almonds for sprinkling

Preheat your oven to 350°F and grease a 9-by-13-inch baking pan with nonstick spray.

Whisk together the flour, baking powder, baking soda, salt, cinnamon, and cardamom in a large bowl. Whisk to combine. In a medium bowl, mix together the oil, honey, sugars, eggs, tea, lemon juice, and bourbon (if using). Once the wet ingredients are fully whisked together, pour into the flour mixture and mix to incorporate fully. You can do this by hand with a whisk, or in a stand mixer fitted with a paddle attachment.

Pour the batter into your prepared pan and sprinkle with the slivered almonds. Bake for 20 to 30 minutes, until the center of the cake barely springs back to the touch and the edges of the cake are barely coming away from the pan.

This is served great warm, or at room temperature. Because of the high sugar and liquid content, this cake lasts really well and will still be delicious after about a week kept at room temperature. You can also freeze it in slices and pull it out when you want a piece of delicious honey cake!

Angela Says

* For the gluten-free flour, I recommend Bob's Red Mill Gluten Free 1 to 1 Baking Flour (518 g).

* For a more intensely flavored cake, use 1 cup (240 ml) of brewed coffee instead of tea.

DATE + LEMON CAKE

The humble date cake, soft and intensely flavored, perfect with a cup of tea. It always reminds me of one of my very best friends, Tuesday—it was one of the first cakes she tried at Goldenrod and, to this day, is the cake she still asks about whenever she visits the shop. We made one for her 30th birthday, to travel all the way from us in Nebraska to her home in Los Angeles.

It may not be the most gorgeous cake in this book, but it deserves our time because it really is one of the most delicious.

YIELD

One 9-by-13-inch cake

INGREDIENTS

Nonstick spray for pan

4 cups (700 g) Medjool dates

Zest and juice of 3 lemons

2½ cups (240 g) almond flour

½ cup (120 ml) melted coconut oil

1 teaspoon ground cinnamon

½ teaspoon sea salt

2½ teaspoons baking soda

6 large eggs

½ cup (75 g) sliced almonds

Preheat your oven to 350°F. Spray a 9-by-13-inch baking pan with nonstick spray and line with a piece of parchment paper. I like to cut the piece of parchment about 12 inches long, so it extends out and across the width of the pan, so you can lift out the cake when it's done.

Combine the pitted dates and the lemon zest and juice in a food processor. Process on high speed until it's a smooth puree. You'll have to stop the machine, open it, and scrape down the sides a few times through this process to get the mixture nice and smooth.

Transfer the puree to the bowl of a stand mixer fitted with the paddle attachment. Add the almond flour, coconut oil, cinnamon, salt, baking soda, and eggs. Mix on low speed until completely combined, about 1 minute.

Pour into your prepared pan and scatter the sliced almonds on top. Bake for about 30 minutes, or until a paring knife inserted into the center comes out clean.

Remove from the oven and let cool completely before lifting it out of the pan. Be sure you run a knife around the edges of the cake before you pull it out! I like to cut this very small squares—it's very rich and keeps well for about 6 days at room temperature.

Angela Says

✳ This is a pretty unconventional batter, but you'll know it's right when it looks like a light and fluffy cake batter. The reaction of the baking soda and lemon juice helps with that.

✳ You can make the batter several days in advance, or even store it in your fridge to bake on demand.

✳ This bakes well in any shape! As you can see in this photo, we used a mini loaf pan to make little individual cakes, but you can choose a round cake pan as well.

BLUEBERRY BUCKLE
WITH PECAN STREUSEL

This is a riff on my favorite coffee cake my mom made when I was growing up—plus blueberries! The pecan streusel is so good, you should double it and use it on top of muffins, or baked in between layers of a pound cake. It's that good! Her version wasn't dairy-free and gluten-free, but this recipe lends itself very well to both. I added ground cardamom to her original recipe as well, because I can't leave well enough alone. You'll note a rather unusual mixing method for this cake—the basis for this came from a very old recipe, and I'd just hate to complicate something that has worked well for so long.

This is something I can see myself wrapping up in a piece of parchment paper and eating on my way to work. Or also during a meeting. Never a bad time for blueberry cake with streusel.

YIELD

One 9-inch square cake

CAKE

2 cups (250 g) all-purpose flour or 2 cups gluten-free all-purpose flour

¾ cup (150 g) granulated sugar

2½ teaspoons baking powder

1 teaspoon sea salt

4 tablespoons (½ stick, 55 g) unsalted butter, at room temperature, or ¼ cup (48 g) vegetable shortening

¾ cup (180 ml) milk, almond milk, or your favorite dairy-free milk

1 large egg

1 teaspoon ground cardamom

1 cup (150 g) fresh or frozen blueberries

STREUSEL

1 cup (179 g) light brown sugar

2 teaspoons ground cinnamon

¼ cup (60 ml) melted coconut oil

¾ teaspoon sea salt

¾ cup (90 g) pecans, chopped

Preheat your oven to 350°F. Spray a 9-inch square baking dish with nonstick spray.

Make the cake: Place all the cake ingredients, except the blueberries, in the bowl of a stand mixer fitted with the paddle attachment, and mix on low speed to combine. Then, increase the mixer speed to medium-high and mix for about 1 minute. Fold in the blueberries. Set aside.

Make the streusel: Mix together all the streusel ingredients in a small bowl. This should hold together like wet sand. If you need to add a bit more sugar or oil to make it that consistency, please do!

To assemble, layer half of the cake batter on the bottom of your prepared pan, then sprinkle with half of the streusel, followed by the rest of the batter, then the rest of the streusel.

Bake for about 45 minutes, or until the center of the cake doesn't give at all when you poke and a paring knife or toothpick inserted into the cake comes out clean.

Angela Says

＊For the gluten-free flour, I recommend Bob's Red Mill Gluten Free 1 to 1 Baking Flour (296 g).

NECTARINE COBBLER

This is the last-minute, use-every-fruit-in-the-fridge recipe you've been waiting for. You'll be the star of your party, or your home. And yes, it might be a little confusing when you read through the recipe and see that the batter goes on the bottom of the pan, fruit on top—but the photo shows batter on top and fruit on the bottom. Thus is the magic of baking! The cobbler batter is truly cakelike and it soaks up juice from the fruit. My favorite part, no doubt, is the edge, where the juice and the cake meet the pan.

I make this recipe with nectarines but you can absolutely make this with berries, plums, cranberries, pears, even mango would be really fun. I'd steer clear of apples, though, as the cake will be finished baking before the apples are soft and luscious.

YIELD

One 9-inch-square cobbler

INGREDIENTS

Nonstick spray for pan

5 nectarines, chopped into 1- to 2-inch pieces

½ cup (100 g) granulated sugar

¼ cup (30 g) cornstarch or tapioca starch

2 tablespoons fresh lemon juice

2 cups (250 g) all-purpose flour or 2 cups gluten-free all-purpose flour

1 tablespoon baking powder

1 teaspoon sea salt

1 tablespoon ground cardamom

6 tablespoons (90 ml) melted coconut oil

1½ cups (360 ml) milk, almond milk, or your favorite nondairy milk

1 large egg or flax egg (page 30)

Angela Says

✱ For the gluten-free flour, I recommend Bob's Red Mill Gluten Free 1 to 1 Baking Flour (296 g).

✱ Change this up by omitting the cardamom and adding something else you love. I recommend ground cinnamon, lemon zest, or even a handful of chocolate chips (vegan if necessary).

✱ Glaze with some pure maple syrup or honey (go with the syrup if you need to bake vegan) right after it comes out of the oven, to give your cobbler a professional-looking shine.

Preheat your oven to 400°F. Spray a 9-by-9-by-4-inch baking pan with nonstick spray.

You'll need two bowls. In the first, combine the fruit, ¼ cup (50 g) of the sugar, and the starch and lemon juice. Turn the fruit around a few times with a spoon until evenly coated with the starch and sugar. Set aside.

In the second bowl, whisk together the flour, baking powder, salt, and cardamom. Next, pour in the oil, milk, and egg. Whisk to combine. It's okay if this batter is a little lumpy.

Pour the batter into the bottom of your prepared pan, then knock in the sugary-starchy fruit on top. Sprinkle with a little extra sugar if you'd like. Bake for about 45 minutes, or until the edges are brown and crispy, the fruit is bubbling up a little, and the center of the cobbler-cakey part doesn't give back at all when you poke it.

Serve this hot, cold, or room temperature. I like to imagine my Grandma Helen pouring a little milk or cream over it in a bowl and eating it with a tiny antique dessert spoon.

BASE MUFFIN + VARIATIONS

There are many different kinds of muffin people. I am a muffin person who loves to find texture and pieces of things inside a muffin. I want to find little pockets of fruit and crunches of nuts or coconut throughout the little cake. This is a great recipe that, if you'd like to, you can customize with your favorite ingredients.

I made a couple of suggestions for additions in this recipe, but do something that *you* love. Keep solid piece additions to about 2 cups total, and any liquid additions (such as lemon juice) to ½ cup maximum. I am a firm believer in sprinkling the top of each muffin with a little granulated sugar. It's the perfect finishing touch.

YIELD

8 large muffins or
16 small muffins

INGREDIENTS

4 tablespoons (½ stick, 55 g) unsalted butter, at room temperature, or ¼ cup (48 g) vegetable shortening

½ cup (100 g) granulated sugar, plus 2 tablespoons (25 g) for sprinkling

4 large eggs

1 teaspoon sea salt

2½ cups (313 g) all-purpose flour or 2½ cups gluten-free all-purpose flour

2 teaspoons baking powder

1 teaspoon pure vanilla extract

1 cup (240 ml) milk, almond milk, or your favorite nondairy milk

Preheat your oven to 350°F. Line 8 large wells or 16 small wells of a muffin pan with store-bought paper liners or make your own from parchment paper.

Combine your choice of fat and ½ cup (100 g) of the sugar in the bowl of a stand mixer fitted with the paddle attachment. Mix on medium speed with a paddle attachment to cream together the two ingredients. Next, add the eggs, one at a time, making sure to mix well after each addition. The mixture may look a little separated after you add all the eggs—that is okay. You want it all as well combined as possible, but sometimes it does look a little broken. Add the salt, flour, baking powder, and vanilla and mix on low speed to incorporate. Slowly start streaming in the milk while the mixer is running. Once you have added all the milk, increase the speed to make sure you work out any lumps of shortening or flour in the mixture. Remove the bowl from the mixer and fold in any additions at this time.

Fold in additional ingredients, such as fruit and nuts (if using), once your batter is fully mixed and complete. I like to be sure to keep my fruit pieces intact, so gently folding them in at the end is key.

Portion the muffin batter evenly among the prepared muffin wells. Sprinkle with the remaining ¼ cup (50 g) of sugar. Bake for 18 to 25 minutes, depending on the size of your muffins. The muffins are done when they are a nice golden brown color and the centers of each muffin do not give at all when you press them lightly. You can also insert a cake tester or paring knife to make sure it comes out clean.

Serve warm!

Angela Says

✱ For the gluten-free flour, I recommend Bob's Red Mill Gluten Free 1 to 1 Baking Flour (370 g) or King Arthur Gluten Free Measure for Measure Flour (300 g).

✱ Muffins are always best with a little hint on top of what you'll find inside. Save a tiny bit of your add-in ingredients to add to the top of your muffins, with a tiny sprinkle of sugar. It adds a great finishing touch.

MUFFIN VARIATIONS

RASPBERRY + COCONUT

Fold in 1 cup (100 g) shredded sweetened or unsweetened coconut and 1 cup (150 g) frozen or fresh raspberries to your finished Base Muffin batter. Save a little bit of coconut and one raspberry for each muffin to garnish on top. Sprinkle with sugar before baking.

APPLE + MAPLE + PECAN

Fold in ¼ cup (40 g) pure maple syrup (we love Grade B syrup!), 1 cup (160 g) chopped fresh applies, and ½ cup (62 g) chopped, raw pecans to your finished Base Muffin batter. Sprinkle with sugar before baking.

TARTS + PIES + SQUARES

I dove fearlessly into making tarts when I was about 16.
At this point, I spent hours at the big bookstore in town, poring over the French Laundry's relatively new cookbook. I didn't know what a Michelin-starred restaurant was, what most of the terminology in their book meant, and I certainly didn't know how to make any of it—and I was absolutely captivated by all of it. It was around this time I stayed up all night on weekends to make all of the recipes I was copying down into my baking notebooks at the bookstore.

Peanut butter truffles. Grape jelly pâte de fruit. And the French Laundry's famous Lemon Sabayon-Pine Nut Tart with Honeyed Mascarpone Cream. I had written down verbatim every step of how to make this tart and had memorized how it was supposed to look. All of this was new to me: pressing the pine nut crust into the tart pan, whipping eggs and sugar over a pot of boiling water, letting the tart brown *just enough* under the oven's broiler. It was deeply satisfying to cut slices of this tart and plate it with a giant dollop of the sweet cream. I had no idea what I was getting into with that recipe, but by then I was completely hooked on tarts and more important, trying every recipe that I didn't understand.

This chapter will help you test the waters on tarts with crusts that you press into the pan, no rolling out delicate dough required. These are the pie recipes to keep in your back pocket for holidays, for pie-eating contests, and for when you are just craving a nice big slice. I was intimidated to start making pies because my mom has always been the pie matriarch in my family, with perfectly cooked crusts and fillings, and the most delicately crimped edges. Then, I just started trying to make them. With each pie, I learned what they need more and less of, and how I could improve my crimping. Know that your crimping will just keep getting more beautiful and that you will keep finding your own style the more pies and tarts you make.

Squares are the casual sister to pies, tarts, and cakes. They are baked in a vessel that you can travel with, store them in, and serve from. I'm usually guilty of being the person who keeps taking little slivers off the edge of the square in a communal pan, eventually eating an entire square. I love to invite my friends to help themselves, choosing a size that they want, from the part of the pan they prefer. I enjoy seeing and experiencing the seasons through square flavors and colors.

CHOCOLATE GANACHE TART
WITH COOKIE CRUST

Tarts were one of the first things I really got into when I started to bake. They always look impressive, but really are just a cinch to make. Don't be intimidated by this! I promise, you really can press this simple cookie crust into the pan, and it will look incredible. The hardest part of a chocolate ganache filling for me has always been the patience it takes to wait while the chocolate sets. I always want to dive right in. Your patience will be rewarded.

Think of it this way: all you have to do is use your fingers to press the crust into a pan, bake it, then whisk together hot chocolate and milk and pour it into the crust. Let's go!

YIELD

One 11-inch tart

COOKIE CRUST

Nonstick spray for pan

1½ cups (144 g) almond flour

1½ cups (186 g) all-purpose flour or 1½ cups gluten-free all-purpose flour

⅓ cup (30 g) unsweetened cocoa powder

¼ cup (50 g) granulated sugar

1 teaspoon sea salt

8 tablespoons (1 stick, 112 g) unsalted butter or ½ cup (96 g) vegetable shortening

3 tablespoons cold water

CHOCOLATE GANACHE FILLING

2 cups (310 g) chopped bittersweet chocolate or chips, vegan if necessary

1 teaspoon sea salt

2 teaspoons instant coffee granules

1½ cups (360 ml) milk, almond milk, or your favorite nondairy milk

1 cup (240 ml) melted coconut oil

Preheat your oven to 375°F and spray a standard 11-inch fluted tart pan with nonstick spray.

Make the cookie crust: Place the almond flour, baking flour, cocoa powder, sugar, and salt in the bowl of a stand mixer fitted with the paddle attachment and mix on low speed to combine the ingredients. Add your choice of fat and mix again on low speed to break up the fat into pea-size pieces. Slowly add the cold water and mix until the dough has formed a nice ball. Press the dough into the prepared pan, using your hands, making sure the crust is an even thickness across the bottom and up the sides of the pan. Bake for about 20 minutes, or until the crust no longer looks shiny but has a matte finish and is slightly coming away from the sides of the pan. Remove from the oven and set aside to cool at room temperature.

Make the ganache filling: Combine the chocolate, salt, and instant coffee granules in a heatproof medium bowl. Heat the milk in a small saucepan until it just begins to simmer. Turn off the heat and carefully pour the milk into the bowl of chocolate. Let the ingredients sit for about 2 minutes, then mix together gently with a whisk. Once the milk and chocolate have melted together and the mixture is a silky, beautiful chocolate, add the melted coconut oil and gently whisk again to combine.

Gently pour the chocolate ganache into the prepared tart crust, making sure to have an even layer of ganache across the top of the tart. Let the tart sit at room temperature until the ganache is set, about 2 hours. Then, you can transfer the tart to the refrigerator to finish setting. Let the tart set in the fridge for at least 3 hours before serving.

Angela Says

✱ Don't touch the tart for a couple of hours after you pour in the ganache filling. If you move the tart too soon when the filling hasn't set completely, the ganache may get a little wrinkly on top. Be patient and move it to your refrigerator after the entire 2-hour wait time.

✱ For the gluten-free flour, I recommend Bob's Red Mill Gluten Free 1 to 1 Baking Flour (222 g).

POMEGRANATE TART

Using pomegranate juice in addition to lemon juice in this tart gives a slightly sweeter and less tart citrus flavor than lemon alone. The result is a gorgeous dessert that is unconventional, but totally appropriate for a holiday. I recommend using gelatin sheets in this pomegranate curd recipe because it adds some stability to the filling, meaning that you can cut through the tart in a really clean line without the filling spilling out at all. If you don't mind a less firm filling, feel free to make this without the gelatin.

YIELD
One 11-inch tart

CRUST
Nonstick spray for pan

1¼ cups (156 g) all-purpose flour or 1¼ cups gluten-free all-purpose flour

1⅓ cups (124 g) almond flour

⅓ cup (67 g) granulated sugar

1 teaspoon sea salt

8 tablespoons (1 stick, 112 g) unsalted butter, at room temperature, or ½ cup (96 g) vegetable shortening

⅓ cup (80 ml) cold water

POMEGRANATE CURD

2 gelatin sheets (optional)

1 cup (240 ml) pomegranate juice

½ cup (120 ml) fresh lemon juice

1½ cups (300 g) granulated sugar

1 teaspoon sea salt

7 large eggs

7 large egg yolks

¾ cup (180 ml) melted coconut oil

2 drops red gel food coloring

Angela Says

✳ For the gluten-free flour, I recommend Nu Life Always Gluten Free All-Purpose Flour (169 g) or Bob's Red Mill Gluten Free 1 to 1 Baking Flour (185 g).

✳ Be sure to let your tart set completely in the fridge before serving! And I know it can be tempting to speed up the process by putting it into the freezer, but this won't work out well in the long run. Just be patient.

Preheat your oven to 400°F and spray an 11-inch fluted tart pan with nonstick spray.

Make the crust: Combine the flour, almond flour, sugar, and salt in a large bowl. Add your choice of fat and use a fork to break it into pea-size pieces. Add the water and mix with the fork to combine. The mixture should be supple, well combined, without any flecks of dry ingredients. Use your hands to gently press the tart dough into your prepared pan. Be sure to get into the bottom edge all the way around and up the sides of the pan. Place the tart pan on a sheet pan and chill in the freezer for about 15 minutes before baking.

Bake the tart crust directly from the freezer for about 25 minutes, or until the edges start to brown and the dough has gone from a shiny finish to a bit more matte finish. Remove from the oven and set aside to cool at room temperature while you prepare the curd.

Make the curd: Fill a small bowl with ice water and add the gelatin sheets, one by one (if using). Pour the lemon and pomegranate juices into a medium saucepan, then add the sugar, salt, eggs, and egg yolks. Whisk to combine completely. Place over medium-low heat and whisk the mixture constantly, making sure to reach your whisk to the bottom and corners of the pot. The curd will start out thin, but will slowly start to thicken. After about 10 minutes, the curd will be very thick and a few bubbles will start popping up. Remove the pot from the heat. Add the coconut oil and red food coloring and whisk well to combine. Pull the gelatin sheets out of the ice water, squeeze out the excess water, and add these to the pot of curd, whisking again to combine until the gelatin is dissolved in the curd.

Pour the finished curd into the cooled tart crust. Using an offset spatula or the back of a spoon, spread the curd to the edges of the crust.

Gently transfer your tart to the refrigerator and let cool completely, or for about 4 hours before serving.

RICE CUSTARD TART

My mom made a super-creamy, not-too-sweet rice custard when we had leftover rice from the night before. It was one of her dad's favorite desserts that she passed on to have us enjoy, too. Along with the rice, she filled the custard with raisins and a pinch of cinnamon, and topped it off with a sprinkle of nutmeg. It was something I always looked forward to, and could never stop eating.

Here's my revamped version, in a nice almond flour tart crust. A great way to use up leftover rice—and a great way to find a new dessert addiction.

YIELD

One 11-inch tart

CRUST

Nonstick spray for pan

1¼ cups (156 g) all-purpose flour or 1¼ cups gluten-free all-purpose flour

1⅓ cups (125 g) almond flour

⅓ cup (67 g) granulated sugar

1 teaspoon sea salt

8 tablespoons (1 stick, 112 g) unsalted butter or ½ cup (96 g) vegetable shortening

⅓ cup (80 ml) cold water

RICE CUSTARD FILLING

3 large eggs

One 15-ounce (424 g) can full-fat coconut milk

1 teaspoon pure vanilla extract

½ teaspoon ground cinnamon

1 cup (175 g) cold cooked rice

½ cup (75 g) raisins

¼ teaspoon sea salt

¼ cup (30 g) powdered sugar for dusting

Preheat your oven to 400°F and spray an 11-inch fluted tart pan with nonstick spray.

Make the crust: Combine the flour, almond flour, sugar, and salt in a large bowl. Add your choice of fat and use a fork to break the pieces of fat into pea-size pieces. Add the water and mix with the fork to incorporate. The mixture should be supple and well combined, without any flecks of dry ingredients. Use your hands to gently press the tart dough into your prepared tart pan. Be sure to get into the bottom edge all the way around, and up the sides of the pan. Place the tart pan on a baking sheet pan, and chill in the freezer for about 15 minutes before baking.

Place the tart pan, still on its baking sheet, in the oven directly from the freezer and bake for about 25 minutes, or until the edges start to brown and the dough has gone from a shiny finish to a bit more matte finish. Remove from the oven and set aside to cool at room temperature while you prepare the custard filling.

Make the custard filling: Whisk together the eggs, coconut milk, vanilla, and cinnamon in a bowl. Add the cooked rice, raisins, and salt and mix again to combine.

Keeping the tart pan on the baking sheet, pour the filling into the prebaked tart crust. Transfer the tart pan to your oven, baking sheet and all, and bake for about 30 minutes, or until the filling is set—the center of the custard shouldn't move when you lightly jiggle the pan.

Remove from the oven and allow to cool at room temperature, then let the tart cool in the fridge for at least 1 hour before serving.

*For the gluten-free flour, I recommend Nu Life Always Gluten Free All-Purpose Flour (169 g) or Bob's Red Mill Gluten Free 1 to 1 Baking Flour (185 g).

*I recommend using day-old rice, but you can make it the same day, just let it cool before using.

CHEESECAKE
WITH ALMOND + WALNUT CRUST

This cheesecake comes together quickly and with a few simple tips (see Angela Says), you'll be making cheesecake for friends and family, and of course yourself. The nuttiness of the crust is a really smart pairing with the tart cream cheese filling—and happens to be a great gluten-free alternative. If you prefer a graham crust, use the recipe from the Mini Lime Pies (page 165). Each of our staff members at Goldenrod gets to choose a birthday dessert for themselves and, even though we offer to make any pastry under the sun, this cheesecake is one of the most popular birthday treats they choose. We serve it topped with Goldenrod's Favorite Lemon Curd (page 236), Chocolate Oven Ganache (page 232), and my favorite is actually Classic Vanilla Buttercream (page 223) and lots of berries.

YOU
DO **YOU**

MAKE THIS

⊔ vegan
⊔ dairy-free
✗ gluten-free
✗ traditional

YIELD

One 9-inch cheesecake

CRUST

1½ cups (144 g) almond flour

1 cup (95 g) walnuts, roughly chopped

¼ cup (50 g) granulated sugar

½ teaspoon sea salt

⅓ cup (80 ml) melted coconut oil

FILLING

1½ (8-ounce [225 g]) packages cream cheese, at room temperature (340 g total)

¾ cup (150 g) granulated sugar

1 teaspoon sea salt

2 teaspoons pure vanilla extract

1 teaspoon fresh lemon juice

3 large eggs

1 large egg yolk

¼ cup (80 g) sour cream

Preheat your oven to 325°F. Spray a 9-inch round cake pan with nonstick spray and line with a piece of parchment paper cut to fit the bottom.

Make the crust: Combine the almond flour, walnuts, sugar, and salt in a small bowl. Pour in the coconut oil and mix to incorporate. Press in an even layer into the bottom of the prepared cake pan. Bake for about 15 minutes, or until the crust is a nice golden brown. Remove from the oven and set aside.

Make the filling: Be sure your cream cheese is at room temperature before beginning. If you are short on time, you can warm it for about 10 seconds on the stove or in the microwave. Put it in the bowl of a stand mixer fitted with the paddle attachment and mix on medium-high speed for 3 to 5 minutes, until the cream cheese is soft, fluffy, and there aren't any lumps. Add the sugar, salt, vanilla, and lemon juice and mix again to combine. Add the eggs and egg yolks, one at a time, mixing well after each addition. If you start with room-temperature cream cheese, the mixture won't need to be mixed for too long. This is good!

Pour the filling over the cooled crust, smoothing the top to make an even layer. Bake for 50 to 60 minutes, until the filling moves as one unit with a gentle tap on the side of the pan. Remove from the oven and let cool at room temperature for about 1 hour, then transfer to the refrigerator to finish cooling, about 5 hours.

To unmold, use a paring knife to go around the edge of the pan, between the cheesecake and the pan. Heat the bottom of the pan held above the burner of your stove, or dip the bottom of the pan in a bowl of boiling water for about 7 seconds. Unmold upside-down onto a plate, tapping to fully release. Set another plate on the bottom of the cheesecake and flip again to put the cheesecake upright on the second plate. Top with berries, melted chocolate, or nothing at all.

Angela Says

✳ The most common concern I hear is that people don't want their cheesecake to crack on top. To prevent that:

Make sure your cream cheese is at room temperature before you use it. Softening cream cheese in a mixer creates a lot of air that gets worked into the mixture, especially when you add the eggs. That air expands in the oven and makes the cheesecake puff up on top before the center is cooked completely, so that puffed layer falls back down on the center, which causes cracks. I think that cracks don't ruin cheesecakes, and that berries piled high in the center will make you forget there was ever a crack at all.

Bake your cheesecake at a lower temperature. Be patient, and don't plan to leave the house for at least 2 hours after you start baking the cheesecake.

GRAHAM CRACKER CREAM PIE

This recipe is very close to my heart. We spent a lot of time eating with my mom's side of the family while growing up. That meant my grandmother, Helen Cariotto; my uncle, John Cariotto; his wife, Penny; and their three kids, plus my parents and siblings. We had big family dinners every Sunday night, rotating between my parents' house and my aunt's and uncle's house. My Grandma Helen always held court at the head of the table.

When we did go out to a restaurant to eat, we went to a place called the Pantry. It had two very quaint locations with lots of dark stained wood, brown leather benches, and dark orange and brown stained-glass lamps.

The Pantry had a tall, rotating pie case. It was full of fruit pies, lemon meringue pie, French silk pie, and the one and only graham cracker cream pie. My cousin, Chris, and I loved this pie. Perfect for vanilla lovers. Perfect for whipped cream lovers.

Graham cracker cream pie: A perfect pie with a sugary graham cracker crust, a healthy layer of vanilla custard, and an incredibly tall, delicately whipped pile of very sweet whipped cream.

It's arguably the best pie in the world. I had to make my own version. Not only to have a dairy-free pie so I can eat it, but as a reminder of the times we spent around those dark brown tables at the Pantry, going on for hours telling jokes and slurping up the last bubbles of Green River soda.

YOU DO YOU

MAKE THIS

- ✗ vegan
- ✗ dairy-free
- ✗ gluten-free
- ✗ traditional

YIELD

One 9-inch pie

GRAHAM CRACKER CRUST

Nonstick spray for pan

2 cups finely ground graham cracker crumbs (gluten-free, vegan, and/or dairy-free if necessary)

⅓ cup (167 g) granulated sugar

¼ teaspoon sea salt

7 tablespoons (100 ml) melted coconut oil

VANILLA CUSTARD

1 cup (240 ml) milk, almond milk, or your favorite nondairy milk

1 cup (240 ml) canned full-fat coconut milk

¼ cup (30 g) cornstarch or tapioca starch

½ cup (100 g) granulated sugar

2 teaspoons pure vanilla extract

Pinch of turmeric to add a slight yellow color

TOPPINGS

1 recipe Whipped Coconut Cream (page 230)

Graham crackers (gluten-free, vegan, and/or dairy-free if necessary) for garnish (optional)

Preheat your oven to 400°F and spray a 9-inch pie pan generously with nonstick spray.

Make the crust: Combine the graham cracker crumbs, sugar, and salt in a medium bowl. Add the melted coconut oil and continue mixing with a fork to combine. The mixture should be the texture of wet sand. Press the piecrust into the prepared pie pan, making sure to reach the top edges of the pan. Bake until the whole crust is a nice golden brown, 12 to 15 minutes. Remove from the oven and let it cool completely at room temperature.

Make the custard: Combine the milk, coconut milk, starch, granulated sugar, vanilla extract, and turmeric in heavy-bottomed pot. Whisk well and make sure there are no lumps of starch. Place the pot over medium-low heat and whisk the custard constantly until it has a thick consistency, about 10 minutes. You should be able to see the trails the whisk leaves in the custard when it is done cooking. Remove from the heat and pour the hot custard directly into the baked and cooled piecrust. Spread evenly so the custard has a nice, flat top. Place a piece of plastic wrap directly on the surface of the custard and refrigerate for at least 2 hours.

Top the cooled custard with the Whipped Coconut Cream. Add some store-bought graham cracker pieces to the top of your coconut cream swoop, if you desire. Serve cold and store in the refrigerator for up to 4 days.

STRAWBERRY PRETZEL PIE

What's not to love? A sweet and salty pretzel base, fresh strawberries barely held together with their own juices, and a whipped coconut cream topping. This is something I remember eating during the peak of hot Nebraska summers. I always tried to scrape more than my fair share of the salty pretzels on the bottom.

This was a very popular dish in the 1990s in Nebraska—a really popular potluck and summer holiday menu item. It was always called a "salad" though, which I thought was a little odd, so I made it into a pie. But, if we're calling this a salad, I'd like to see more salads just like this!

YIELD

One 9-inch pie

PRETZEL CRUST

Nonstick spray for pan

6 cups (400 g) pretzels, dairy- or gluten-free if necessary

3 tablespoons sugar

5 tablespoons (75 ml) melted coconut oil

STRAWBERRY FILLING

4 cups (476 g) fresh strawberries, hulled and quartered

1 cup (240 ml) water

¾ cup (150 g) granulated sugar

3 tablespoons cornstarch or tapioca starch

Red gel food coloring as desired

TOPPING

1 recipe Whipped Coconut Cream (page 230)

Make the crust: Grease a 9-inch pie pan with nonstick spray. Crush the pretzels with the bottom of a pot or with a rolling pin until they are a mixture of pretzel powder and pretzel pieces. Transfer the pretzels to a bowl, add the sugar and coconut oil, and mix together to combine. Press into the bottom of the prepared pie pan and transfer to your refrigerator. Let the crust chill and set while you make the filling.

Make the filling: Crush 1 cup (120 g) of the strawberries and cook in a small saucepan with the water for about 5 minutes. Strain through a fine-mesh strainer and let the juice cool for about 20 minutes. Combine the sugar and starch in a small bowl and whisk into the strained berry juice. Transfer back to the saucepan and cook, stirring constantly, until thickened and bubbly. Add a couple of drops of red food coloring as desired. Place 1½ cups (178 g) of the remaining strawberries in the bottom of your chilled piecrust, then pour *half* of the sauce over the berries. Repeat those layers with the last 1½ cups (178 g) of strawberries and the remaining sauce. Chill for at least 5 hours before serving.

Top with Whipped Coconut Cream and serve.

Angela Says

✳ If you want to garnish with a few fresh pretzels like I have in this photo, please add them just before serving. These will become soft if refrigerated!

MINI LIME PIES

These are fun and festive little tarts for small gatherings. It always feels so special when you have a dessert all to yourself. While I am a huge fan of sharing things family style, sometimes you just want to do something a little cuter. These are just the ticket! With a dollop of Whipped Coconut Cream (page 230) on top, these are everyone's little tart dream come true.

I recommend using gelatin sheets in this lime curd recipe because it adds some stability to the filling, meaning that you can cut through the tart in a really clean line without the filling spilling out at all. If you don't mind a less firm filling, feel free to make this without the gelatin.

YIELD

8 mini tarts

CRUST

Nonstick spray for pans

2½ cups (313 g) all-purpose flour or 2½ cups gluten-free all-purpose flour

¾ cup (134 g) light brown sugar

1 teaspoon sea salt

½ teaspoon ground cinnamon

4 tablespoons (½ stick, 55 g) unsalted butter, at room temperature or ¼ cup (48 g) vegetable shortening

¾ cup (180 ml) melted coconut oil

3 tablespoons honey

LIME CURD

1 gelatin sheet (optional)

⅔ cup (160 ml) fresh lime juice

¾ cup (150 g) granulated sugar

1 teaspoon sea salt

4 large eggs

4 large egg yolks

¼ cup (60 ml) melted coconut oil

Drop of green gel food coloring

TOPPING

Whipped Coconut Cream (page 230)

Preheat your oven to 375°F. Select eight mini pie pans, each 4 inches wide and 1 inch deep. Spray with nonstick spray and set aside while you make the crust.

Make the crust: Combine the flour, brown sugar, salt, and cinnamon in a medium bowl. Add your choice of fat and cut it into the dry mixture with a fork until the fat is in pea-size pieces. Add the melted coconut oil and honey and mix with a fork to combine. The mixture should be the texture of wet sand.

Divide the crust equally among the prepared mini tart pans and, using your fingers, press the mixture into an even crust, across the bottom and up the sides of the pans. Bake for about 12 minutes, or until the crust is just barely golden brown. Remove from the oven and set aside to cool.

Make the curd: Place the gelatin sheet (if using) in a bowl of ice-cold water and let it bloom in the water while you make the rest of the curd. Combine the lime juice, sugar, salt, eggs, and egg yolks in a medium heavy-bottomed pot and whisk together vigorously. Once the mixture is well combined, place the pot over medium heat and whisk the mixture constantly, being sure to reach the bottom and edges of the pot. After about 10 minutes, the mixture will be very thick and bubbly. Turn off the heat. Lift the gelatin sheet from the cold water and squeeze out any excess water. Add the gelatin sheet, coconut oil, and a drop or two of green food coloring to the mixture and whisk to combine.

Transfer the finished curd to a liquid measuring cup so you can easily pour it into the finished tart crusts. Fill the crusts up to the top edge and transfer to the fridge to set and completely cool.

Finish with a little dollop of Whipped Coconut Cream.

Angela Says

✱ For the gluten-free flour, I recommend Nu Life Always Gluten Free All-Purpose Flour (338 g) or Bob's Red Mill Gluten Free 1 to 1 Baking Flour (370 g).

LEMON MERINGUE PIE

Lemon meringue pie was always my Grandma Helen's favorite pie, so it always reminds me of her. The tart lemon curd perfectly contrasts with the rich flakiness of the crust. The ethereal lightness of adding a cooked Swiss meringue to this pie is otherworldly.

I won't lie to you, you'll want to make this on a day when you have time for a project. It takes a few more steps than most of my recipes, but the payoff is great. If you want to put on a show for your friends, pull out your blowtorch when they arrive so they can watch you add the finishing, smoky touch to this dessert.

YIELD

One 9-inch pie

CRUST

1 recipe Goldenrod's Favorite Piecrust (page 169)

LEMON CURD

1 gelatin sheet (optional)

1 cup (240 ml) fresh lemon juice

1¼ cups (250 g) granulated sugar

1 teaspoon salt

4 large eggs

4 large egg yolks

½ cup (120 ml) melted coconut oil

TOPPING

1 recipe Marshmallow Swiss Meringue (page 226)

Preheat your oven to 350°F and have ready a 9-inch pie pan.

Make the crust: Prepare the Goldenrod Favorite Piecrust dough as directed. If using the gluten-free version of this dough, press it into your pie pan with floured fingers. If using the traditional recipe, roll it into a 14-inch circle on a floured work surface. Gently lay the crust in the pan, gently pressing it to fit in the bottom corners of the pan. Trim off all but 1 inch of excess dough from around the outside edge of the pan. Tuck the edge under itself and gently crimp it with your fingers, or press gently with the tines of a fork. Prick the bottom and sides of the piecrust with a fork.

Bake just until the edges start to turn brown, for 14 minutes. Remove from the oven and set aside to cool while you prepare the lemon curd.

Prepare the lemon curd: Place the gelatin sheet (if using) in a bowl of ice water and let it bloom while you make the rest of the curd. Combine the lemon juice, sugar, salt, eggs, and egg yolks in a heavy-bottomed pot. Whisk together vigorously before heating. Once the mixture is well mixed, place the pot over medium heat. Whisk the mixture constantly, being sure to reach the bottom and edges of the pot. After about 10 minutes, the mixture will be very thick and bubbly. Turn off the heat and add the coconut oil. Squeeze any excess water from your soaked gelatin sheet, and add that to the pot as well. Whisk to combine.

Pour the lemon curd directly into the prebaked piecrust and spread evenly with the back of a spoon or with an offset spatula. Place a piece of parchment paper or plastic wrap directly on the surface of the lemon curd and transfer gently to your refrigerator to cool for about 2 hours, or until fully chilled and set.

Prepare the Marshmallow Swiss Meringue: Start making your meringue once the lemon curd is fully set in the piecrust.

Remove the lemon curd-filled crust from the refrigerator, remove the parchment paper or plastic wrap from the surface of the curd, and begin to delicately dollop the finished meringue on top. Be as creative as you like with this.

Once you have finished dolloping to your delight, it's time to torch the meringue. You can use either a blowtorch, or a preheated broiler set to its highest temperature, for 45 to 60 seconds. Either way, use caution and keep a close eye on your meringue. You wanted toasted, not burned, edges.

Keep refrigerated until serving. I recommend serving this within 2 hours of adding the meringue.

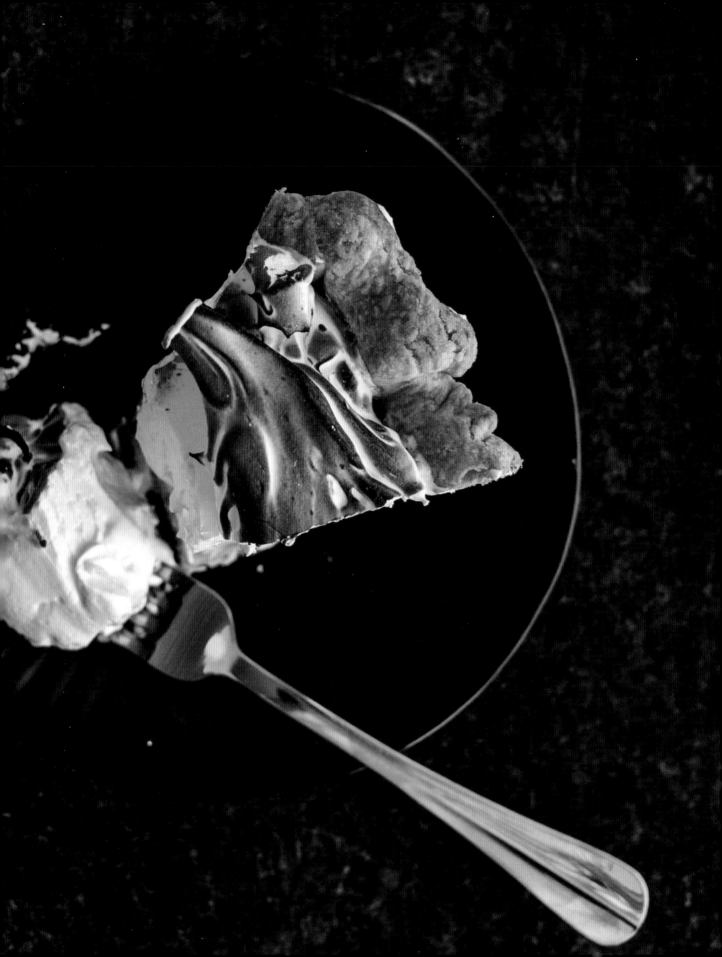

GOLDENROD'S FAVORITE
PIECRUST

This is the last piecrust recipe you will ever need. I watched my mom make pies with ease my entire life, so intricate instructions for making, using, and storing piecrusts never made sense to me. She would pull together a piecrust in minutes, use it right away with no time to let it rest—or would let it sit at room temperature, uncovered, for hours, and then use it whenever she got around to it.

It took me a little time to understand this recipe, mostly because I tried to overcomplicate it. Go with your gut, follow these simple instructions, and you, too, can have perfect pies every time.

And, we only have to substitute one ingredient (the flour) to take this from simply a delicious vegan piecrust, to a wonderful piecrust that is both vegan *and* gluten-free.

Follow along, and don't be scared!

YOU DO YOU

MAKE THIS

✗ vegan

✗ dairy-free

✗ gluten-free

✗ traditional

YIELD

One piecrust (bottom of pie only)

INGREDIENTS

1½ cups (188 g) all-purpose flour or 1½ cups gluten-free all-purpose flour

1 teaspoon sea salt

½ cup (96 g) vegetable shortening

¼ cup (60 ml) cold water

Combine the flour, salt, and shortening in a medium bowl. Use a fork to break up the shortening in the flour until the fat is in pea-size pieces. Slowly add in the cold water, mixing everything together with the fork. Keep adding the water slowly, and mixing until the dry ingredients come together easily with your hands. The dough will be a little shaggy—that is good! Gather it all together with your hands to make a loose ball of dough.

You can knead it one or two times on your work surface to pull the dough together, but don't work it more than that. If the dough feels a little wet and is sticking to the counter, add a bit of the appropriate flour to the outside. If it feels a little dry, add a few drops of cold water.

This dough can sit at room temperature for an hour or two until you need to use it—and can benefit from some time to rest. You can also make it well in advance and wrap it well and tight, then store in the refrigerator until you are ready to use it.

✳ For the gluten-free flour, I recommend King Arthur Gluten Free Measure for Measure Flour (180 g).

✳ The gluten-free version of this dough should be pressed into your pie pan with your fingers, whereas the version with gluten needs to be rolled out with a rolling pin. In either case, dust with plenty of the appropriate flour to prevent the dough from sticking to your hands, or to the rolling surface.

✳ We make all of our pies with a bottom crust only and opt for other toppings, such as streusel, or pies that don't need toppings or a top crust!

APPLE PIE WITH OAT STREUSEL

All great bakers need an apple pie recipe in their back pocket. Here is mine. The maple syrup gives a nice consistency to the syrupy, luscious apple filing. I prefer my apple pie with unpeeled apples, but you are welcome to peel yours if the texture doesn't work for you.

YIELD

One 9-inch pie

CRUST

1 recipe Goldenrod's Favorite Piecrust (page 169), plus appropriate flour for dusting

APPLES

6 Granny Smith or Jonathan apples

1 teaspoon ground cinnamon

2 teaspoons ground cardamom

½ cup (60 g) cornstarch or tapioca starch

½ cup (80 g) pure maple syrup

½ cup (89 g) light brown sugar

1 teaspoon sea salt

STREUSEL TOPPING

1 cup (179 g) light brown sugar

1½ cups (188 g) all-purpose flour or 1½ cups gluten-free all-purpose flour

¾ cup (75 g) rolled oats, certified gluten-free if necessary

1 teaspoon ground cinnamon

1 teaspoon sea salt

6 tablespoons (90 ml) melted coconut oil

Preheat your oven to 350°F and have ready a 9-inch pie pan.

Make the crust: Prepare Goldenrod's Favorite Piecrust dough as directed. If using the gluten-free version of this dough, press it into your pie pan with floured fingers. If using the traditional recipe, roll it into a 14-inch circle on a floured work surface. Gently lay the crust in the pie pan, gently pressing to fit in the bottom corners of the pan. Trim off all but 1 inch of excess dough from around the outside edge of the pan. Tuck the edge under itself and gently crimp it with your fingers, or press gently with the tines of a fork. Prick the bottom and sides of the piecrust with a fork.

Prepare the apples: Slice the apples in ½-inch slices, removing the core and any seeds. No need to peel them, but you can if you prefer that. Combine the sliced apples, cinnamon, cardamom, starch, maple syrup, brown sugar, and salt in a large bowl. Mix together very well so that the spices, sugar, and starch coat the apples well. Let sit for about 30 minutes while you make the streusel and roll out the piecrust.

Prepare the streusel: Combine the brown sugar, flour, oats, cinnamon, salt, and coconut oil in a small bowl. Mix together with a fork. The mixture should gently hold together to form loose clusters, but not be too wet.

Fill the prepared piecrust with your apple mixture, including all the juices! Spread the apples evenly across the piecrust. Pile high with the prepared streusel, forming little clusters as you go. Place the pie on a baking sheet, so the apple juices fall onto that instead of into your oven.

Bake for about 1 hour, or until the crust is a dark golden brown and the juices running from the pie are thick and bubbly. If the juices are still thin, cover the pie with foil and bake for another 15 minutes.

Remove from the oven and let cool completely at room temperature before serving.

Angela Says

✳ For the gluten-free streusel flour, I recommend Nu Life Always Gluten Free All-Purpose Flour (203 g) or Bob's Red Mill Gluten Free 1 to 1 Baking Flour (222 g).

✳ You are welcome to omit the crust and bake this in a 9-by-13-inch baking dish to make a great apple streusel.

BOURBON PECAN PIE

Every Thanksgiving, after I've made hundreds of pies at the bakery, I always hope there will be one extra bourbon pecan pie sitting around by itself at the end of the holiday rush. It's the one pie I want to dive right into with just a fork. I live for the candylike filling; how crispy and gently toasted the sugar and pecans are on the top of the pie; and the delicate crust under the gooey, soft candy filling, and the perfectly flaky and crunchy pie edges. I am guilty of dissecting whatever I am eating, including pie. I will take a piece of the piecrust, dip it into the center of my piece of pie, and make perfect little bites for myself as I go along.

For someone who is obsessed with making perfect bites, full of many different textures, this is the perfect treat.

And even if that isn't you, this is the greatest, simplest pecan pie. Make it with or without the bourbon.

YOU
DO **YOU**

MAKE THIS

❏ vegan

✗ dairy-free

✗ gluten-free

✗ traditional

YIELD

One 9-inch pie

CRUST

1 recipe Goldenrod's Favorite Piecrust (page 169), plus appropriate flour for dusting

FILLING

½ cup (100 g) granulated sugar

½ cup (89 g) light brown sugar

3 tablespoons (45 ml) melted coconut oil

¾ cup (120 g) pure maple syrup

4 large eggs

3 tablespoon bourbon (optional)

2 cups (250 g) pecan pieces

Preheat your oven to 350°F and prepare a 9-inch pie pan by placing it on a 13-by-18-inch baking pan.

Make the crust: Prepare the Goldenrod's Favorite Piecrust dough as directed. If using the gluten-free version of this dough, press it into your pie pan with floured fingers. If using the traditional recipe, roll it into a 14-inch circle on a floured work surface. Gently lay the crust in prepared pan, gently pressing it to fit in the bottom corners of the pan. Trim off all but 1 inch of excess dough from around the outside edge of the pan. Tuck the edge under itself and gently crimp it with your fingers, or press gently with the tines of a fork. Prick the bottom and sides of the piecrust with a fork.

Bake for about 12 minutes, or until slightly golden brown around the top edges, with a matte, flaky finish on the bottom (it should not be completely baked). Set aside to cool while you make the filling.

Make the filling: Combine the sugars, coconut oil, maple syrup, eggs, and bourbon (if using) in a small bowl. Whisk together vigorously so that everything is well combined.

Place the pecans on the bottom of the partially baked piecrust. Pour the filling over the pecans. Gently transfer the pie on its baking sheet to the oven and bake for about 45 minutes, until the top forms a nice sugary finish and the edge of the piecrust is a medium brown. If your crust seems done and perfectly golden brown before the filling is set, gently cover the crust with foil and allow the pie to continue baking until set.

Remove from the oven and let cool at room temperature for at least 3 hours before serving. Store at room temperature for up to 2 days or in the refrigerator for up to a week.

PUMPKIN PIE
WITH NUT CRUST

It's easy for pumpkin pie to become incredibly rich, cloyingly sweet, and just overall a little too much. Please, let me introduce you to a pumpkin pie that is none of those things! The nut crust is just salty enough to make things interesting. Making this recipe was the first time I really enjoyed this Americana holiday treat. It's delightful and has pleased both pumpkin pie purists and pumpkin pie skeptics alike. Make this the day before you want to eat it. The pumpkin custard needs to set up for a few hours and is even better the second day.

This recipe calls for an almond flour-based crust (see Angela Says).

YIELD

One 9-inch pie

NUT CRUST

Nonstick spray for pan

2 cups (192 g) almond flour

¼ cup (50 g) granulated sugar

1 teaspoon sea salt

⅓ cup (80 ml) melted coconut oil

PUMPKIN CUSTARD

One 15-ounce (424 g) can pure pumpkin puree

½ cup (89 g) light brown sugar

¼ cup (40 g) pure maple syrup

3 tablespoons cornstarch or tapioca starch

¼ cup (60 ml) milk, almond milk, or your favorite nondairy milk

2 tablespoons (30 ml) melted coconut oil

½ teaspoon sea salt

1 teaspoon ground cinnamon

½ teaspoon ground ginger

TOPPING

Whipped Coconut Cream (page 230)

Preheat your oven to 400°F and spray a 9-inch pie pan generously with nonstick spray.

Prepare the crust: Combine the almond flour, granulated sugar, and salt in the bowl of a food processor. Pulse until everything is well mixed. Add the coconut oil and pulse again until incorporated. Press the dough into the prepared pie pan with your fingers, making sure the crust reaches the top edge of the pan.

Bake just until the edges start to turn brown, for 14 minutes. Remove from the oven and set aside to cool while you prepare the pumpkin custard.

Make the custard: Combine the pumpkin puree, brown sugar, maple syrup, and starch in a medium bowl and whisk well. Add the milk, coconut oil, salt, cinnamon, ginger, and cardamom and whisk again to incorporate everything well. Pour the custard into the prebaked pie-crust and spread to the edges of the pan, using a spatula. Bake for about 45 minutes, or until the shine on top of the pie is gone, leaving a matte finish.

Remove from the oven and let the pie cool at room temperature for about 30 minutes before transferring to the refrigerator to firm up for another 4 to 6 hours.

Serve when completely cool, with a healthy dollop of Whipped Coconut Cream.

Angela Says

✳ If you don't have almond flour, or can't have nuts, check out our Graham Cracker Crust (page 161) and use that instead (choosing the vegan and gluten-free options if necessary).

PEAR + CRANBERRY CROSTATA

This is a great option to make when you need a quicker version than a pie. It bakes in a fraction of the time that a full pie does, doesn't require a pie pan, and is endlessly customizable. I am absolutely a crostata person. I like the ratio of crust to filling (almost equal parts!), it's quicker and simpler to make than a pie, and you can pick up a slice and eat it like a piece of pizza.

Cranberry and pear are a great combination. There is the soft sweetness of pear slices, then they're met with the tang and brightness of each little cranberry. If you've been looking for an alternative to the holiday pie world, welcome to the land of crostata.

YOU
DO **YOU**

MAKE THIS

✘ vegan

✘ dairy-free

✘ gluten-free

✘ traditional

YIELD

One 10-inch crostata

INGREDIENTS

6 pears (Anjou or Bosc work well)

1½ cups (150 g) fresh or frozen cranberries, fresh or frozen

¾ cup (150 g) granulated sugar, plus ¼ cup (50 g) for sprinkling crust

1 teaspoon pure vanilla extract

2 teaspoons fresh lemon juice

½ cup (60 g) cornstarch or tapioca starch

¾ teaspoon sea salt

1 recipe Goldenrod's Favorite Piecrust (page 169), plus appropriate flour for dusting

¾ cup (72 g) almond flour

¼ cup (60 ml) milk, almond milk, or your favorite nondairy milk

Angela Says

✘ I add almond flour on the crust, beneath the fruit, to help separate the fruit juice from the crust. We want the crust to stay nice and crisp, and this helps that happen.

Preheat your oven to 400°F and cut a sheet of parchment paper to fit a 13-by-18-inch baking sheet.

Slice the pears into ½-inch slices, being sure to remove the core. Combine the sliced pears, cranberries, sugar, vanilla, lemon juice, starch, and salt in a medium bowl. Mix gently so that all the ingredients are mixed and dispersed well. You want to be sure the starch and sugar are coating the fruit well. Set aside.

Prepare the Goldenrod's Favorite Piecrust dough as directed. If using the gluten-free version of this dough, press it with floured fingers on the sheet of prepared parchment paper. If using the traditional recipe, roll it on the sheet of prepared parchment paper. Make sure the parchment paper is well floured so the dough doesn't stick. The pie dough should be about ⅓ inch thick, and about 18 inches wide. The dough will extend beyond the parchment paper. Transfer the dough, with the parchment paper underneath, to the baking sheet.

Sprinkle the almond flour in the center of the pie dough, then pile the fruit and their juices in the center. Fold over the edges of the pie dough, to hold in the fruit and juices. If you are using the gluten-free dough, you will need to use a bench scraper to pick up the edges of the crust to fold over. Pinch the edges of the dough together to be sure they don't separate during the baking process. Brush the dough with the milk and sprinkle with the remaining 4 tablespoons of sugar.

Bake for about 50 minutes, or until the crust is perfectly golden brown, and the juices bubbling in the center of the crostata are thick. Remove from the oven and let cool at room temperature before serving.

PEACH STREUSEL SQUARES

If you're like me and hoard stone fruit in the summer, never knowing whether it's the last batch of perfect peaches you'll get all summer, this recipe is for you. When you end up with more peaches than you know what to do with, make this recipe. It benefits from overripe fruit, and you can't go wrong with two incredible streusel cookie layers on either side of fresh peach preserves.

YIELD

One 9-by-13-inch pan

FILLING

6 fresh peaches, sliced and pitted

½ cup (89 g) light brown sugar

5 tablespoons cornstarch or tapioca starch

½ cup (120 ml) fresh lemon juice

1 teaspoon sea salt

STREUSEL COOKIE

Nonstick spray for pan

3½ cups (438 g) all-purpose flour or 3½ cups gluten-free all-purpose flour

2¼ cups (447 g) light brown sugar

2¾ cups (247 g) rolled oats, certified gluten-free if necessary

2 teaspoons sea salt

1½ teaspoons ground cinnamon

12 tablespoons (1½ sticks, 167 g) unsalted butter, at room temperature, or ¾ cup (144 g) vegetable shortening

¾ cup (180 ml) melted coconut oil

Preheat your oven to 350°F and spray a 9-by-13-inch baking pan with nonstick spray. Because the peaches in this recipe are pretty sticky, I recommend lining the pan with parchment paper and spraying the paper with nonstick spray as well.

Make the filling: Combine the sliced peaches with the brown sugar, lemon zest, starch, lemon juice, and salt in a bowl. Mix well with a spoon so the sugary syrup coats every piece of peach. Set aside.

Make the streusel cookie: Combine the flour, brown sugar, rolled oats, salt, and cinnamon in a large bowl. Mix together with a fork. Add your choice of fat and use the fork to break it into pea-size pieces within the flour. Add the coconut oil and mix together with the fork to incorporate.

Divide the streusel cookie dough in half. Press half of the dough with your hands into the bottom of your prepared pan. Once it is in an even layer, pour on the peach mixture and spread evenly across the layer of cookie dough. Sprinkle the second half of the cookie dough mixture on top of the peaches.

Bake for 60 to 75 minutes, until the edges are bubbling, the top is golden brown, and when you jiggle the pan a little, the center barely moves. Remove from the oven and let this cool completely in the pan before slicing and serving.

Angela Says

✱ For the gluten-free flour, I recommend Nu Life Always Gluten Free All-Purpose Flour (437 g) or Bob's Red Mill Gluten Free 1 to 1 Baking Flour (518 g).

✱ These became an instant hit at Goldenrod. You can make these with pears, apples, berries, or whatever fruit you have available!

APRICOT + OAT COOKIE SQUARES

These squares are so rich: two layers of a rich, oat-dotted cookie, separated with a gooey, luscious strip of cooked apricots that almost tastes like candy. The cookie is full of walnuts and shredded coconut. I love the subtle saltiness. My mom made a version of these with dates, and it was one of my all-time favorite treats she'd make. She got the recipe from her cousin, Dori. Thanks for sharing the recipe, Mom!

These squares are not for the faint of heart! They pack great for adventuring, wrapped tightly in parchment paper.

YOU
DO **YOU**

MAKE THIS

✗ vegan

✗ dairy-free

✗ gluten-free

✗ traditional

YIELD

One 9-by-13-inch pan

APRICOT FILLING

2 cups (180 g) dried apricots, chopped

1¼ cups (300 ml) water

1 cup (200 g) granulated sugar

OAT COOKIE

Nonstick spray for pan

1 cup (240 ml) melted coconut oil

1 cup (179 g) brown sugar

2 cups (250 g) all-purpose flour or 2 cups gluten-free all-purpose flour

1 cup (90 g) rolled oats, certified gluten-free if necessary

1 teaspoon sea salt

1 teaspoon baking soda + 1 teaspoon warm water

½ cup (50 g) sweetened or unsweetened shredded coconut

1 cup (125 g) crushed walnuts

Preheat your oven to 350°F and spray a 9-by-13-inch baking pan with nonstick spray. Because the apricot layer of this recipe is pretty sticky, I recommend lining the pan with parchment paper long enough to extend from the pan on two sides, for easy lifting, and spraying the paper with nonstick spray as well.

Make the filling: Combine the chopped apricots, water, and granulated sugar in a small pot. Cook over medium heat, stirring often. I like to press down the fruit a little with a spoon to break it up as much as I can. Cook for about 20 minutes, or until it has a jammy consistency. Remove from the heat and set aside to cool a little while you make the cookie.

Make the cookie: Stir together the oil and brown sugar in a large bowl. Next, add the flour, rolled oats, salt, and the baking soda mixture. Mix with a spoon or spatula until incorporated, then add the coconut and walnuts.

Divide the dough in half. Press half of the cookie dough into your prepared pan, making sure it covers the bottom of the pan completely and is in all of the corners and edges. Pour on the slightly cooled apricot mixture and spread evenly over the cookie. Next, sprinkle the second half of the cookie dough over the apricot layer. This layer does not need to be perfectly even.

Bake for about 40 minutes, or until the edges are starting to get bubbly, and the top cookie layer is nice and golden brown. Remove from the oven and let cool completely in the pan, before lifting it out with the parchment paper. Cut into small pieces to share.

Angela Says

✳ For the gluten-free flour, I recommend Nu Life Always Gluten Free All-Purpose Flour (270 g) or Bob's Red Mill Gluten Free 1 to 1 Baking Flour (296 g).

LEMON SQUARES

Everyone needs a lemon square recipe. This recipe keeps a really vibrant yellow color and has a very flaky almond shortbread crust. This is not an ordinary lemon square: we use lemon curd as the filling. It is a super-rich, satisfying lemon curd that you really sink your teeth into. No one will be disappointed if you bring these to a holiday or picnic.

YIELD

One 9-by-13-inch pan

CRUST

Nonstick spray for pan

¾ cup (75 g) powdered sugar

1¼ cups (156 g) all-purpose flour or 1¼ cups gluten-free all-purpose flour

1½ cups (144 g) almond flour

1 teaspoon sea salt

¾ cup (180 ml) melted coconut oil

FILLING

1 recipe Goldenrod's Favorite Lemon Curd (page 236)

Preheat your oven to 350°F and spray a 9-by-13-inch rimmed baking pan with nonstick spray.

Prepare the crust: Whisk together the powdered sugar, flour, almond flour, and salt in a large bowl. Pour in the melted coconut oil and mix with a rubber spatula to incorporate. Once the mixture is thoroughly combined, pour into your prepared pan. Use your hands or an offset spatula to spread the crust evenly across the pan. Make sure your crust is not too thin or too thick in any spots. Bake for about 15 minutes, or until light golden brown. Remove from the oven and set aside to cool.

Add the filling: Prepare Goldenrod's Favorite Lemon Curd. While still hot, pour the curd over your prebaked crust. Spread across the crust to make an even layer, then carefully transfer the pan to the oven.

Bake for about 20 minutes, or until the edges are bubbling and starting to turn brown. Remove from the oven and let cool at room temperature for about an hour before storing in the refrigerator. Serve cold. You can store these in the refrigerator, covered, for about a week.

Angela Says

✱ For the gluten-free flour, I recommend Nu Life Always Gluten Free All-Purpose Flour (169 g) or Bob's Red Mill Gluten Free 1 to 1 Baking Flour (185 g).

COCOA NUTTY SQUARES

We are always trying to think of squares that are packed with texture, are visually appealing, easy to serve and travel with, and are—of course—super seasonally delicious. At the beginning of our holiday season, I wanted to create a really luxe square that captured the decadence of winter. These Cocoa Nutty Squares have a not-too-sweet chocolate cookie crust and a filling packed with nuts and chocolate chips. Once refrigerated, these squares cut like a dream and are a great alterative to classic winter desserts.

YIELD

One 9-by-13-inch pan

COCOA CRUST

Nonstick spray for pan

½ cup (60 g)
powdered sugar

1¼ cups (156 g) all-purpose flour or 1¼ cups gluten-free all-purpose flour

1½ cups (144 g) almond flour

½ teaspoon sea salt

¼ cup (22 g) unsweetened cocoa powder

12 tablespoons (1½ sticks, 167 g) unsalted butter, at room temperature, or ½ cups (120 ml) melted coconut oil

NUTTY FILLING

½ cup (100 g)
granulated sugar

½ cup (89 g)
light brown sugar

½ cup (80 g)
pure maple syrup

4 large eggs

4 tablespoons (½ stick, 56 g) unsalted butter, at room temperature, or ¼ cup (60 ml) melted coconut oil

¾ cup (94 g) walnuts

¾ cup (94 g) pecans

½ cup (78 g) dark chocolate chips, dairy-free if necessary

Preheat your oven to 350°F and prepare a 9-by-13-inch rimmed baking pan with nonstick spray.

Prepare the crust: In a mixing bowl, whisk together the powdered sugar, flour, almond flour, salt, and cocoa powder in a large bowl. Pour in the melted coconut oil and mix with a rubber spatula to incorporate. Once the mixture is thoroughly combined, pour it into your prepared pan. Use your hands or an offset spatula to spread the crust evenly across the pan. Make sure your crust is not too thin or too thick in any spots. Bake for about 15 minutes, or until light golden brown. Remove from the oven and set aside to cool.

Prepare the filling: Whisk together the sugars, maple syrup, and eggs in a medium bowl. Add the coconut oil and whisk gently to thoroughly incorporate. Set aside.

Sprinkle the walnuts, pecans, and chocolate chips across the crust, to form a nice even layer. Evenly pour the prepared filling on top. Gently transfer the pan to the oven and bake for about 30 minutes, or until the center doesn't jiggle when you shake the pan gently.

Let cool completely at room temperature, then transfer to the fridge to store. These cut best when they are cold. Enjoy at any temperature.

Angela Says

✳ For the gluten-free flour, I recommend Nu Life Always Gluten Free All-Purpose Flour (169 g) or Bob's Red Mill Gluten Free 1 to 1 Baking Flour (185 g).

✳ Toasted nuts are usually the way to go for baking because they impart so much flavor. However, we use raw nuts in this recipe because they get nice and toasted while the squares bake. If you start with toasted nuts, your squares can end up tasting almost too toasted.

✳ If you don't have the exact ratio of nuts listed here, no worries! Just use the nuts you have on hand. The only important rule is that you use the same total quantity listed above, but you can use any combination and ratio of the nuts you have and love.

B.A.B.E. SQUARES

BadAss Babes Everywhere (B.A.B.E.) Squares are named for the team of women I work with at Goldenrod Pastries, and for the community of strong women who lift up and support one another. This square is my love song to strong babes everywhere. It has a flaky chocolate cookie crust, a healthy layer of dark chocolate ganache, and a rich terrain of chocolate crumble on top.

These squares comes together with a few steps that can be made relatively quickly. You just need to plan for a couple of hours of refrigeration time before serving. Make the B.A.B.E. squares for your best friends. It's a treat that stands out among slices of cake, cookies, and cupcakes.

YIELD

One 9-by-13-inch pan, about 18 squares

CRUST

Nonstick spray for pan

½ cup (60 g) powdered sugar

1¼ cups (156 g) all-purpose flour or 1¼ cups gluten-free all-purpose flour

1½ cups (144 g) almond flour

½ teaspoon sea salt

¼ cup (22 g) unsweetened cocoa powder

½ cup (120 ml) melted coconut oil

GANACHE FILLING

1⅛ cups (270 ml) milk, almond milk, or your favorite nondairy milk

1¾ cups (271 g) dark chocolate chips or chopped chocolate, vegan if necessary

¼ teaspoon sea salt

¾ cup (180 ml) melted coconut oil

DARK CHOCOLATE CRUMBLE

½ cup (63 g) all-purpose flour or ½ cup gluten-free all-purpose flour

⅓ cup (59 g) light brown sugar

½ cup (45 g) unsweetened cocoa powder

¼ teaspoon sea salt

1 teaspoon instant coffee powder

¼ cup (60 ml) melted coconut oil

Preheat your oven to 350°F and spray a 9-by-13-inch rimmed baking pan with nonstick spray.

Prepare the crust: Whisk together the powdered sugar, flour, almond flour, salt, and cocoa powder in a large bowl. Pour in the melted coconut oil and mix with a rubber spatula to incorporate. Once the mixture is thoroughly combined, pour it into your prepared pan. Use your hands or an offset spatula to spread the crust evenly across the pan. Make sure your crust is not too thin or too thick in any spot. Bake for about 15 minutes, or until light golden brown. Remove from the oven and set aside to cool.

Prepare the ganache filling: Heat the milk in a heavy-bottomed saucepan over medium heat. Place the chocolate chips and salt in a large heatproof bowl. Once the milk starts to simmer, remove from the heat and pour it over the chocolate chips and salt. Let sit for 2 minutes, then stir gently until all the chocolate is melted and the mixture is shiny and luxurious. Add the melted coconut oil and mix again to combine. Pour the ganache directly over the baked crust. Let cool at room temperature.

Make the dark chocolate crumble: Line a baking sheet with parchment paper. Combine the flour, brown sugar, cocoa powder, salt, and instant coffee powder in a medium bowl. Add the coconut oil and stir with a spoon to incorporate. You should have a nice crumble consistency that is not too wet and has various crumble sizes. Spread evenly on the prepared baking sheet and bake for about 15 minutes. The baked crumble will have a very matte finish. Remove from the oven and let cool completely at room temperature.

Finish the squares: You want the ganache to be set, but still be a little tacky on top when you sprinkle it with the crumble. Sprinkle with the crumble after the squares have been at room temperature for about 1 hour. Make sure the crumble evenly covers the entire surface of the squares. Refrigerate for about 2 hours before serving.

Angela Says

✱ For the gluten-free flour, I recommend Nu Life Always Gluten Free All-Purpose Flour (169 g) or Bob's Red Mill Gluten Free 1 to 1 Baking Flour (185 g).

✱ Add fresh raspberries to the top of the squares, intermixed with the dark chocolate crumble. They add color, texture, and a little pop of tartness.

✱ You can make all three components up to 1 week ahead of time. Store the crust in your freezer, store the crumble at room temperature, and store the ganache filling in an airtight container in your refrigerator. To assemble, reheat the ganache filling gently over the stove or in the microwave until it has a pourable consistency. Follow the instructions in the original recipe to finish the squares.

PARTY CAKES

Angela Says

✳ Any of the cake batters in this chapter can also be baked as cupcakes. They will bake for 20 minutes in a 350°F oven.

Celebrating is what we do at Goldenrod Pastries. It's a frame of mind! I don't know whether I became obsessed with celebrations because I like making cakes, or whether I like making cakes because I'm obsessed with celebrations, and celebrating for no reason. While I was growing up, instead of having a few large, extravagant parties every year, we would have lots of small parties. Parties for no reason, and parties for seemingly small things, such as to celebrate taking a test and finishing a week at marching band camp. My mom started us on celebrations from a young age. They weren't modest by any measure, but they were all homespun.

We at Goldenrod have had the honor to make cake for an incredible range of celebrations, including births, anniversaries, last day at work, first day at a new job, marriage, divorce . . . the list goes on. To be present in any way for these enormous life events never stops feeling special. What I do notice is that people usually order cakes for others, or sometimes people come in to order a cake for themselves, feeling a little silly. I love when you throw yourself a party! Make yourself a cake or order yourself a cake, but always celebrate the moments in your life that deserve the celebration.

Celebrate everything. And do it with cake if you can.

This is just a selection of some of my very favorite party cakes. Eat them with gusto. Eat them with friends. Celebrate without reservation.

YELLOW CAKE WITH DARK CHOCOLATE BUTTERCREAM

This is such a classic combination. It's one of the most festive-looking cakes. It satisfies your chocolate lovers, and your vanilla lovers. The color of the deep, rich yellow cake with dark chocolate frosting is something special—not to mention how great a dash of rainbow sprinkles makes it look.

This version of yellow cake is so incredibly tender. It holds up just the right amount to the tines of your fork, while just letting you dive right in.

YIELD

One 2-layer 9-inch round cake, serves about 12 people

INGREDIENTS

Nonstick spray for pan

½ pound (2 sticks, 225 g) unsalted butter, at room temperature, or 1 cup (192 g) vegetable shortening

1½ cups (300 g) granulated sugar

4 large eggs

2 large egg yolks

2½ teaspoons baking powder

1 teaspoon sea salt

2 teaspoons pure vanilla extract

3 cups (375 g) all-purpose flour or 3 cups gluten-free all-purpose flour

1 cup (240 ml) milk, almond milk, or your favorite nondairy milk

1 recipe Dark Chocolate Buttercream (page 225)

Angela Says

✳ For the gluten-free flour, I recommend Bob's Red Mill Gluten Free 1 to 1 Baking Flour (444 g).

✳ For more information on baking, cooling, and decorating cakes, refer to Tips for Cakes (page 39).

Preheat your oven to 350°F. Spray two 9-inch round cake pans with nonstick spray and line with parchment paper.

Combine your choice of fat and the sugar in the bowl of a stand mixer fitted with the paddle attachment. Mix on medium speed for about 1 minute. Add the eggs and egg yolks, one at a time, mixing well after each addition. Once the mixture is well combined, add the baking powder, salt, vanilla, and flour. Start your mixer on the lowest speed and gradually stream in the milk. Once everything is combined, increase the speed to medium-high to work out any lumps of flour, scraping the bowl as needed.

Divide the cake batter evenly between the two prepared pans and smooth out the tops. Bake for about 40 minutes, or until the edges of the cake are pulling away from the sides of the pan and the center barely gives back when you gently press it with your finger.

Remove from the oven and let the cakes cool in their pans at room temperature. Once they are cool, use a serrated knife to gently slice off the rounded tops of each cake, transfer the layers to a serving plate, and layer with Dark Chocolate Buttercream.

You can serve the cake immediately, or keep it refrigerated for up to 2 days before serving it.

STRAWBERRY CAKE

This is one of the most popular cakes we make at Goldenrod. I remember while I was growing up, having strawberry cakes that contained strawberry-flavored extract to give it both a distinct strawberry flavor and a pink hue. We opt for a different approach at Goldenrod, sticking to a vanilla cake base and working in fresh strawberries. Adding the chopped strawberries at the beginning of the mixing process allows the berries to be muddled in the mixing bowl with the eggs and sugar. This brings out a lot of strawberry flavor, as well as imparting a slight pinkness to the rest of the batter. Sometimes, we add a drop or two of pink gel food coloring to enhance that strawberry color, but it isn't essential.

If you find some berries at the back of your fridge that you think are a bit overripe to eat, this cake is perfect for them. The softness of very ripe strawberries, plus the release of additional sugars as they ripen, makes them ideal for this cake.

YOU DO YOU

MAKE THIS

✗ vegan
✗ dairy-free
✗ gluten-free
✗ traditional

YIELD

One 3-layer 8-inch or one 2-layer 9-inch round cake, serves about 12 people

INGREDIENTS

6 large eggs or flax eggs (page 30)

2⅔ cups (533 g) granulated sugar

1½ cups (153 g) fresh strawberries, hulled and chopped

1½ cups (360 ml) vegetable oil

1½ tablespoons baking powder

½ teaspoon sea salt

1 teaspoon pure vanilla extract

4½ cups (562 g) all-purpose flour or 4½ cups gluten-free all-purpose flour

1½ cups (360 ml) milk, almond milk, or your favorite nondairy milk

1 drop of pink gel food coloring (optional)

1 recipe Strawberry Buttercream (page 225)

Preheat your oven to 375°F. Spray three 8-inch or two 9-inch round cake pans with nonstick spray and line with parchment paper.

Place the eggs, sugar, and chopped strawberries in the bowl of a stand mixer fitted with the paddle attachment. Mix on medium speed for about 1 minute, or until well combined. Add the vegetable oil, baking powder, salt, and vanilla and mix again to incorporate, 2 minutes. Add all the flour and reduce the mixer speed to low. Once the flour is partially incorporated, stream in about half of the milk, allow it to incorporate slowly, then turn the mixer speed to high; use this time to work out any lumps of flour. Once the lumps are out, reduce the mixer speed to low and slowly stream in the rest of the milk, turning off the mixer just before all the milk is incorporated. Remove the bowl from the mixer, add the food coloring (if using), and fold in any milk that isn't quite incorporated. We do this last step by hand to prevent the batter from being overmixed.

Divide the batter evenly among the prepared cake pans and smooth out the tops. Bake for about 40 minutes, or until the edges of the cake are pulling away from the sides of the pan and the center barely gives back when you gently press it with your finger.

Remove from the oven and let the cakes cool in their pans at room temperature. Once they are cool, use a serrated knife to gently slice off the rounded tops of each cake, transfer the layers to a serving plate, and layer with Classic Strawberry Buttercream.

You can serve the cake immediately, or keep it refrigerated for up to 2 days before serving it.

Angela Says

✳ For the gluten-free flour, I recommend Pamela's Gluten-Free All-Purpose Flour (540 g).

✳ For more information on baking, cooling, and decorating cakes, refer to Tips for Cakes (page 39).

✳ Save your most beautiful strawberries to adorn the top of your cake and use the less perfect, even bruised, fruit to go in the cake layers.

HUMMINGBIRD CAKE

I hadn't heard of hummingbird cake until a few years ago. It is traditionally from the southern part of the United States and how I've gone most of my life without knowing about it is beyond me! The cake itself is a banana base, but when you fold in chopped pineapple and pecans, it takes on a whole new taste. The fruit and nuts add great textural and flavor variation throughout the cake layers.

This is traditionally served with a cream cheese frosting, but we always layer it with either cinnamon or vanilla buttercream at the shop. Hummingbird cake has quickly become one of our favorites, and our customers', too.

YIELD

One 3-layer 8-inch or one 2-layer 9-inch round cake, serves about 12 people

Angela Says

✳ For the gluten-free flour, I recommend Pamela's Gluten-Free All-Purpose Flour (360 g).

✳ For more information on baking, cooling, and decorating cakes, refer to Tips for Cakes (page 39).

✳ You can also bake this in a 9-by-13-inch pan to take away the work of layering the cake.

INGREDIENTS

Nonstick spray for pans

4 ripe medium bananas

2 cups (400 g) granulated sugar

3 large eggs or flax eggs (page 30)

1 cup (240 ml) vegetable oil

1 teaspoon ground cinnamon

Zest of 1 lemon

1 teaspoon sea salt

1 teaspoon baking soda

2 teaspoons baking powder

3 cups (375 g) all-purpose flour or 3 cups gluten-free all-purpose flour

1 cup (225 g) chopped fresh pineapple

1 cup (125 g) pecans, chopped

1 recipe Classic Vanilla Buttercream (page 223) or Cinnamon Buttercream (page 225)

Preheat your oven to 375°F. Spray three 8-inch or two 9-inch round cake pans with nonstick spray and line with parchment paper.

Combine the bananas and sugar in the bowl of a stand mixer fitted with the paddle attachment. Mix on medium speed for about 1 minute, or until the bananas are smashed together with the sugar and no large chunks of banana remain. Add the eggs and vegetable oil and mix again to combine well, 2 minutes. Next, add the cinnamon, lemon zest, salt, baking soda, baking powder, and flour and reduce the mixer speed to low. Once the flour is almost completely incorporated, increase the mixer speed to medium-high speed and let it run for a few seconds to remove any lumps of flour. Be careful not to overmix! Remove the bowl from the mixer and fold in the chopped pineapple and pecans, folding from the bottom of the bowl to the top to be sure all ingredients are well incorporated.

Divide the batter evenly among the prepared cake pans and smooth out the tops. Bake for about 30 minutes, or until the edges of the cake are pulling away from the sides of the pan and the center barely gives back when you gently press it with your finger.

Remove from the oven and let the cakes cool in their pans at room temperature. Once they are cool, use a serrated knife to gently slice off the rounded tops of each cake, transfer the layers to a serving plate, and layer with either Classic Vanilla Buttercream or Cinnamon Buttercream.

You can serve the cake immediately, or keep it refrigerated for up to 2 days before serving it.

CONFETTI CAKE
WITH VANILLA BUTTERCREAM

Your quintessential party cake! She is the life of the party and everyone wants a piece. She is dotted with rainbow sprinkles and covered in fluffy buttercream, and is primed and ready for birthday candles, singing, laughing, and celebration.

We love the feeling confetti cake gives you, the excitement of even just the sound of the words together: *confetti cake*. This is one of our most popular cakes at the bakery. Goldenrod is synonymous with joy and we want you to always remind yourself that you, yourself, are worthy of a celebration. People are so giddy when they order a confetti cake. Celebrate yourself, celebrate others.

YIELD

One 3-layer 8-inch round cake, serves about 12 people

INGREDIENTS

Nonstick spray for pans

6 large eggs or flax eggs (page 30)

2⅔ cups (533 g) granulated sugar

1½ cups (160 ml) vegetable oil

1½ tablespoons baking powder

½ teaspoon sea salt

1 teaspoon pure vanilla or almond extract

4½ cups (562 g) all-purpose flour or 4½ cups gluten-free all-purpose flour

1½ cups (360 ml) milk, almond milk, or your favorite nondairy milk

2⅓ cups (420 g) rainbow jimmy or nonpareil sprinkles, vegan if necessary

1 recipe Classic Vanilla Buttercream (page 223)

Angela Says

✳ For the gluten-free flour, I recommend Pamela's Gluten-Free All-Purpose Flour (540 g).

✳ For more information on baking, cooling, and decorating cakes, refer to Tips for Cakes (page 39).

✳ I also like to add fresh berries between the layers of cake: chop up some strawberries or raspberries if you want to add a little tartness in the middle of the sweet layers of cake.

Preheat your oven to 375°F. Spray three 8-inch round cake pans with nonstick spray and line with parchment paper.

Combine the eggs and sugar in the bowl of a stand mixer fitted with the paddle attachment. Mix on medium speed for about 1 minute, or until well mixed. Add the vegetable oil, baking powder, salt, and vanilla and mix again to combine well, 2 minutes. Add all the flour and reduce the mixer speed to low. Once the flour is partially incorporated, stream in about half of the milk and allow it to incorporate slowly, then increase the mixer speed to high; use this time to work out any lumps of flour. Once the lumps are out, reduce the mixer speed back to low and slowly stream in the rest of the milk, turning off the mixer just before all the milk is incorporated. Remove the bowl from the mixer and fold in ⅓ cup (60 g) of the sprinkles and any remaining milk. We do this last step by hand to prevent the batter from being overmixed.

Divide the batter evenly among the prepared cake pans and smooth out the tops. Bake for about 40 minutes, or until the edges of the cake pull away from the sides of the pan and the center barely gives back when you gently press it with your finger.

Remove from the oven and let the cakes cool in their pans at room temperature. Once they are cool, use a serrated knife to gently slice off the rounded tops of each cake, transfer the layers to a serving plate, and layer with Classic Vanilla Buttercream.

To cover the sides of the cake in sprinkles, use one hand to hold the base of the cake (on a plate), and the other hand to scoop sprinkles on the sides of the cake. I like to do this over a big mixing bowl to catch excess sprinkles.

You can serve the cake immediately, or keep it refrigerated for up to two days before serving it.

COCONUT CAKE
WITH MARSHMALLOW FROSTING

I love coconut cake. Especially when it has so much coconut in it that you really can't tell whether you are eating cake or eating coconut. This recipe is delicious and densely coconutty. Share it with your friends who are looking for a special cake, something out of the ordinary.

The marshmallow frosting on this cake is light, airy, angelic—but is strong enough to hold up the layers of cake. Take this to the next level with a heavy dose of sweetened, shredded coconut around the outside. It hides any imperfections and gives us the final touch of angel wings that this cake deserves.

Our just desserts.

YIELD

One 3-layer 8-inch or one 2-layer 9–inch round cake, serves about 12 people

INGREDIENTS

Nonstick spray for pans

6 large eggs or flax eggs (page 30)

2⅔ cups (533 g) granulated sugar

1½ cups (160 ml) vegetable oil

1½ tablespoons baking powder

½ teaspoon sea salt

1 teaspoon pure vanilla extract

4½ cups (562 g) all-purpose flour or 4½ cups gluten-free all-purpose flour

1½ cups (360 ml) milk, almond milk, or your favorite nondairy milk

1½ cups (150 g) sweetened shredded coconut, plus 2½ cups (225 g) for finishing

1 recipe Marshmallow Swiss Meringue (page 226)

Preheat your oven to 375°F. Spray three 8-inch or two 9-inch round cake pans with nonstick spray and line with parchment paper.

Combine the eggs and sugar in the bowl of a stand mixer fitted with the paddle attachment. Mix on medium speed for about 1 minute, or until well mixed. Add the vegetable oil, baking powder, salt, and vanilla and mix again to combine well, 2 minutes. Add all the flour and reduce the mixer speed to low. Once the flour is partially incorporated, stream in about half of the milk. Allow the milk to incorporate slowly, then increase the mixer speed to high; use this time to work out any lumps of flour. Once the lumps are out, reduce the mixer speed to low and slowly stream in the rest of the milk, turning off the mixer just before all the milk is incorporated. Remove the bowl from the mixer and fold in the shredded coconut and any remaining milk.

Divide the batter evenly between the two prepared pans and smooth out the tops. Bake for about 40 minutes, or until the edges of the cake are pulling away from the sides of the pan and the center barely gives back when you gently press it with your finger.

Remove from the oven and let the cakes cool in their pans at room temperature. Once they are cool, use a serrated knife to gently slice off the rounded tops of each cake, transfer the layers to a serving plate, and layer with Marshmallow Swiss Meringue or Classic Vanilla Buttercream.

To cover the sides of the cake in coconut, use one hand to hold the cake (on a plate), and the other hand to gently press handfuls of coconut on the sides of the cake. I like to do this part over a big mixing bowl to catch excess coconut.

You can serve the cake immediately, or keep it refrigerated for up to 2 days before serving it.

Angela Says

✳ For the gluten-free flour, I recommend Pamela's Gluten-Free All-Purpose Flour (540 g).

✳ For more information on baking, cooling, and decorating cakes, refer to Tips for Cakes (page 39).

CHOCOLATE CAKE
WITH DARK CHOCOLATE BUTTERCREAM

YOU
DO YOU

MAKE THIS

✗ vegan
✗ dairy-free
✗ gluten-free
✗ traditional

This is the chocolate cake you can make when you think you don't have anything on hand to make a chocolate cake. Made from only pantry ingredients, this is a great recipe to keep in your back pocket when you need to make a last-minute cake.

YIELD

One 3-layer 8-inch or 2-layer 9-inch round cake, serves about 12 people

INGREDIENTS

Nonstick spray for pans

4 cups (500 g) all-purpose flour or 4 cups gluten-free all-purpose flour

2 cups (400 g) granulated sugar

2 teaspoons baking soda

1 teaspoon sea salt

¾ cup (68 g) unsweetened cocoa powder

3 cups (720 ml) water

1½ cups (360 ml) vegetable oil

1 tablespoon white distilled or cider vinegar

1 recipe Dark Chocolate Buttercream (page 225)

Preheat your oven to 375°F. Spray three 8-inch or two 9-inch round cake pans with nonstick spray and line with parchment paper.

Whisk together the flour, sugar, baking soda, salt, and cocoa powder in a large bowl. Mix well to combine everything and to remove any lumps. Add the water and vegetable oil and whisk to incorporate. Once everything is well mixed and no lumps of dry ingredients remain, add the vinegar and whisk again to combine.

Divide the batter evenly among the prepared pans and smooth out the tops. Bake for about 40 minutes, or until the edges of the cake pull away from the sides of the pan and the center barely gives back when you gently press it with your finger.

Remove from the oven and let the cakes cool in their pans at room temperature. Once they are cool, use a serrated knife to gently slice off the rounded tops of each cake, transfer the layers to a serving plate, and layer with Dark Chocolate Buttercream.

You can serve the cake immediately, or keep it refrigerated for up to 2 days before serving it.

Angela Says

✳ For the gluten-free flour, I recommend a mixture of 50% Bob's Red Mill Gluten Free 1 to 1 Baking Flour (296 g) and 50% Nu Life Always Gluten Free All-Purpose Flour (270 g) or a mixture of 50% King Arthur Gluten Free Measure for Measure Flour (240 g) and 50% Bob's Red Mill Gluten Free 1 to 1 Baking Flour (296 g).

✳ For more information on baking, cooling, and decorating cakes, refer to Tips for Cakes (page 39).

CHAMPAGNE CAKE
WITH ALMOND BUTTERCREAM

This is one of the most elegant cakes you can present to a party, or to yourself. There is something so satisfying about pouring a glug of Champagne into cake batter. Not only does it add a really delightful flavor, but its bubbles give the cake a little extra lift and buoyancy. This is the taste of quintessential wedding cake, one that truly wouldn't disappoint in any setting.

I added the almond buttercream to top this cake because it truly reminds me of the perfect little slice of nostalgic wedding cake, as it was the flavor of mine and Russell's wedding cake in 2014. Cheers!

YIELD

One 3-layer 8-inch or one 2-layer 9-inch round cake, serves about 12 people

INGREDIENTS

Nonstick spray for pans

6 large eggs or flax eggs (page 30)

2⅔ cups (525 g) granulated sugar

1½ cups (360 ml) vegetable oil

1½ tablespoons baking powder

½ teaspoon sea salt

1 teaspoon almond extract

4½ cups (562 g) all-purpose flour or 4½ cups gluten-free all-purpose flour

¾ cup (180 ml) milk, almond milk, or your favorite nondairy milk

¾ cup (180 ml) sparkling wine or Champagne

1 recipe Classic Almond Buttercream (page 225)

Preheat your oven to 375°F. Spray three 8-inch or two 9-inch round cake pans with nonstick spray and line with parchment paper.

Combine the eggs and sugar in the bowl of a stand mixer fitted with the paddle attachment. Mix on medium speed for about 1 minute, or until well mixed. Add the vegetable oil, baking powder, salt, and almond extract and mix again to combine well, 2 minutes. Add all the flour and reduce the mixer speed to low. Once the flour is partially incorporated, slowly stream in all the milk, allow it to incorporate slowly, then increase the mixer speed to high. Use this time to work out any lumps of flour. Once the lumps are out, lower the mixer speed to low and slowly stream in the sparkling wine, turning off the mixer just before all of the wine is incorporated. Remove the bowl from the mixer and fold in any liquid that isn't quite incorporated. We do this last step by hand to prevent the batter from being overmixed.

Divide the batter evenly among the prepared cake pans and smooth out the top of the cake batter. Bake for about 40 minutes, or until the edges of the cake pull away from the sides of the pan and the center barely gives back when you gently press it with your finger.

Remove from the oven and let the cakes cool in their pans at room temperature. Once they are cool, use a serrated knife to gently slice off the rounded tops of each cake, transfer the layers to a serving plate, and layer with Classic Almond Buttercream.

You can serve the cake immediately, or keep it refrigerated for up to 1 day before serving it. Cheers!

*For the gluten-free flour, I recommend Pamela's Gluten-Free All-Purpose Flour (540 g).

*For more information on baking, cooling, and decorating cakes, refer to Tips for Cakes (page 39).

ORANGE BLOSSOM CAKE
WITH LEMON BUTTERCREAM

We started making this cake right after the Duke and Duchess of Sussex's royal wedding in 2018. Once the flavors of their elderflower and lemon wedding cake had been released to the press, orders started flooding in from customers who were hosting wedding watch parties and wanted their own slices of royal wedding cake. After that weekend, our supply of elderflower essence had dwindled, but we still wanted to continue making a cake that had a really floral flavor. We always kept a bottle of orange blossom water in our supplies, but didn't find too many uses for it—so we decided to try adding it to our cake recipe. We ended up loving it almost more than its elderflower inspiration. This is in our regular rotation now and is absolutely a Goldenrod staff favorite.

YIELD

One 3-layer 8-inch or one 2-layer 9–inch round cake, serves about 12 people

Angela Says

✳ For the gluten-free flour, I recommend Pamela's Gluten-Free All-Purpose Flour (540 g).

✳ For more information on baking, cooling, and decorating cakes, refer to Tips for Cakes (page 39).

✳ I always try to find simple ways to make a fancy cake look fancy in the most natural ways—add edible flower petals, fruit, and maybe even splurge on some gold leaf.

INGREDIENTS

Nonstick spray for pans

6 large eggs or flax eggs (page 30)

2²⁄₃ cups (533 g) granulated sugar

1½ cups (160 ml) vegetable oil

1½ tablespoons baking powder

½ teaspoon sea salt

1 teaspoon orange blossom water

4½ cups (526 g) all-purpose flour or 4½ cups gluten-free all-purpose flour

1½ cups (360 ml) milk, almond milk, or your favorite nondairy milk

1 recipe Lemon Buttercream (page 225)

Preheat your oven to 375°F. Spray three 8-inch or two 9-inch round cake pans with nonstick spray and line with parchment paper.

Combine the eggs and sugar. Mix on medium speed for about 1 minute, or until well mixed. Add the vegetable oil, baking powder, salt, and orange blossom water and mix again to combine well, 2 minutes. Add all the flour and reduce the mixer speed to low. Once the flour is partially incorporated, stream in about half of the milk and allow it to incorporate slowly, then increase the mixer speed to high; use this time to work out any lumps of flour. Once the lumps are out, reduce the mixer speed to low and slowly stream in the rest of the milk, turning off the mixer just before all the milk is incorporated. Remove the bowl from the mixer and fold in any remaining milk. We do this last step by hand to prevent the batter from being overmixed.

Divide the batter evenly among the prepared cake pans and smooth out the tops. Bake for about 40 minutes, or until the edges of the cake pull away from the sides of the pan and the center barely gives back when you gently press it with your finger.

Remove from the oven and let the cakes cool in their pans at room temperature. Once they are cool, use a serrated knife to gently slice off the rounded tops of each cake, transfer the layers to a serving plate, and layer with Lemon Buttercream.

You can serve the cake immediately, or keep it refrigerated for up to 2 days before serving it.

CARROT CAKE
WITH CINNAMON BUTTERCREAM

I first worked on this recipe when I was collaborating on an event with my friend Caroline. She is an incredible pastry chef in New York City and I had been hoping to meet her for years after following her work on social media. I wanted to really wow her with a cake recipe that would be straightforward, incredibly delicious, and could work well with her specialties: big flavors and lots of spices.

This carrot cake recipe comes together so easily with one bowl and a whisk. I love the nostalgic simplicity of the recipe as is, but you can also get creative with the spices you use. I remember Caroline added cardamom, freshly grated ginger, black pepper, and cinnamon.

I hope this simple, delicious, lovely carrot cake finds its way into your cake rotation.

YIELD

One 3-layer 8-inch or one 2-layer 9-inch round cake, serves about 12 people

INGREDIENTS

Nonstick spray for pans

2 cups (358 g) light brown sugar

4 cups (500 g) all-purpose flour or 4 cups gluten-free all-purpose flour

1¾ teaspoons baking soda

4 teaspoons baking powder

1½ teaspoons ground cinnamon

1 teaspoon ground cardamom

1 teaspoon ground ginger

½ teaspoon sea salt

1 cup (240 ml) vegetable oil

3 cups (330 g) grated carrots

3½ cups (840 ml) milk, almond milk, or your favorite nondairy milk

1 tablespoon white distilled or cider vinegar

1 recipe Cinnamon Buttercream (page 225)

Preheat your oven to 375°F. Spray three 8-inch or two 9-inch round cake pans with nonstick spray and line with parchment paper.

Whisk together the brown sugar, flour, baking soda, baking powder, cinnamon, and salt in a large bowl and make sure to whisk well to remove any lumps. Add the vegetable oil and grated carrot and whisk to incorporate. The batter will be very thick at this point. Start adding the milk, about ½ cup (120 ml) at a time, whisking as you go. Once all the milk has been added and is incorporated, add the vinegar and whisk again to combine.

Divide the batter evenly among the prepared cake pans and smooth out the top of the cakes. Bake for about 35 minutes, or until the edges of the cake pull away from the sides of the pan and the center barely gives back when you gently press it with your finger.

Remove from the oven and let the cakes cool in their pans. Once they are cool, use a serrated knife to gently slice off the rounded tops of each cake, transfer the layers to a serving plate, and layer with Cinnamon Buttercream.

You can serve the cake immediately, or keep it refrigerated for up to 2 days before serving it.

Angela Says

✳ For the gluten-free flour, I recommend Bob's Red Mill Gluten Free 1 to 1 Baking Flour (592 g).

✳ For more information on baking, cooling, and decorating cakes, refer to Tips for Cakes (page 39).

ALMOND ROLL CAKE
WITH LEMON CURD

Rolled cakes are meringue based and use very little flour to bind them together, meaning they are incredibly tender and light. This cake ditches flour altogether and uses almond flour instead, which adds a layer of moisture and rich flavor. Sometimes I don't even bother rolling up the cake layer before I dive in with a fork, and you might enjoy that, too. In this case, though, we are rolling it up with some of our very favorite lemon curd. This combination is a Goldenrod staff favorite.

Try out this recipe. It's less challenging than you might think and once you master this, you're on your way to many other kinds of rolled cakes!

YIELD

One 13-inch roll cake

Angela Says

✳ If you don't have two stand mixer bowls, carefully transfer your whipped egg whites to a clean glass or metal bowl. Clean the stand mixer bowl and use it to whip your egg yolks. Or you can whip the egg whites by hand using a clean glass or metal bowl and a whisk.

INGREDIENTS

Nonstick spray for pan

9 large eggs, separated

¼ teaspoon sea salt

1 cup (200 g) granulated sugar

1 teaspoon almond extract

1 teaspoon baking powder

2¼ cups (216 ml) almond flour

½ cup (65 g) sliced almonds

Powdered sugar for sprinkling

½ recipe Goldenrod's Favorite Lemon Curd (page 236)

Combine the egg yolks and the remaining ¾ cup (150 g) of the granulated sugar in a clean stand mixer bowl and whisk vigorously on high speed until they are pale in color and very thick, about 5 minutes. The mixture will form ribbons on top of itself when you lift the whisk up over the bowl. Add the almond extract, baking powder, and almond flour and mix to incorporate.

Fold the whites into the egg yolk mixture with a rubber spatula, starting with about one-quarter of the whites and incorporating them fully to lighten the mixture. Then, add the rest of the whites and gently fold all together until homogenous but still fluffy.

Pour the batter into your prepared pan. Spread evenly with a spatula and sprinkle the top of your cake with the sliced almonds. Bake for about 20 minutes, or until the top of the cake is nice and golden brown and the cake barely springs back when you press it gently with your finger.

Remove from the oven and let the cake cool in the pan for about 5 minutes. Sprinkle a clean kitchen towel generously with powdered sugar. Tip the cake out of its pan onto the prepared towel, remove the parchment paper from the cake, and, using the towel as your guide, roll up the cake, towel and all. We do this right away so that the cake holds its shape when you roll it up with curd inside later. Let the cake cool the rest of the way rolled up in the towel.

Once the cake has cooled, unroll it. Spread a thin layer of lemon curd over the cake and roll it up again—this time, without the towel.

Serve your rolled cake right away, dusted with a little powdered sugar, or keep it refrigerated, covered, for up to 2 days.

Preheat your oven to 350°F. Spray a 13-by-18-inch baking sheet with nonstick spray and line with a piece of parchment paper cut to fit the bottom of the pan.

Place your egg whites and the salt in the bowl of a stand mixer fitted with a whisk attachment, or whisk them by hand using a whisk and a large glass or metal bowl. Whisk, starting on medium-low speed and increasing to high, until they are completely foamy, adding ¼ cup (50 g) of the granulated sugar. Continue to whisk until soft peaks form. The peaks will stand up on their own, but will still look shiny and luscious. Set aside.

CARDAMOM CAKE
WITH PISTACHIO STREUSEL +
STRAWBERRY-ROSE GLAZE

This has gone on and off the menu at Goldenrod, but it always is incredibly popular when it's on! My standard line is that cardamom is interesting enough for people to notice it and be intrigued, but not overwhelming. It's a warm spice—and the combination of this with rose is traditional in a lot of Persian desserts. When I first started making this cake at the birth of my dairy-free baking adventures, I wanted to find ways to color food naturally, and I wanted all of my treats to still be vibrant and interesting looking. So, I started using freeze-dried fruit, pulsed into a fine powder in my glazes and buttercreams.

I was making this for an event in New York a few years ago, and my dear friend Mindy let me use her home kitchen. I made an extra cardamom cake for her young children, Leo and Penny. Not totally sure if they'd enjoy a cardamom cake, we were both thrilled to see them eat it up! One of my favorite baking memories.

YIELD
One 8-inch round cake

PISTACHIO STREUSEL

¾ cup (105 g) chopped raw, unsalted pistachios, divided

⅓ cup (89 g) light brown sugar

1 teaspoon ground cardamom

¼ cup (60 ml) melted coconut oil

CARDAMOM CAKE

Nonstick spray for pan

2 cups (250 g) all-purpose flour or 2 cups gluten-free all-purpose flour

1 teaspoon sea salt

1 teaspoon baking powder

1 teaspoon ground cardamom

1 cup (200 g) granulated sugar

½ cup (120 ml) melted coconut oil or vegetable oil

1⅓ cups (320 ml) canned coconut milk

STRAWBERRY-ROSE GLAZE

⅓ cup (80 ml) coconut milk

1 cup (28 g) freeze-dried strawberries, crushed

1 teaspoon rosewater

½ cup (60 g) powdered sugar

Preheat your oven to 350°F and grease an 8-inch round cake pan. Set aside.

Prepare the streusel: Pulse ½ cup (70 g) pistachios in a food processor with the brown sugar, cardamom, and coconut oil. Set aside while you make the cake batter.

Prepare the cake: Combine the flour, salt, baking powder, cardamom, and granulated sugar in a medium bowl. Using a whisk, make sure everything is well mixed. Add the oil and milk and whisk to combine. If making this with all-purpose flour, be sure not to overmix—but do get out all the clumps. Pour half of the batter into your prepared pan, layer evenly with the pistachio streusel, then spread the remaining batter on top of the streusel. Once evenly spread, bake on the center oven rack for about 35 minutes, or until a paring knife inserted into the center comes out clean. Remove from the oven and set aside to cool for about 10 minutes before removing from the cake pan.

Prepare the glaze: Don't bother cleaning out your food processor between the streusel and this glaze.

Pile your coconut milk, freeze-dried berries, rosewater, and powdered sugar into the food processor, then process on high speed until everything is smooth, pink, and beautiful.

Pour the glaze over your cooled cake and sprinkle remaining ¼ cup (35g) of pistachios around the edge of the cake. This will keep at room temperature for about 5 days. I recommend enjoying it before then, though!

Angela Says

* For the gluten-free flour, I recommend Bob's Red Mill Gluten Free 1 to 1 Baking Flour (296 g).

* This batter should be super smooth and easy to pour. If it feels a little thick, add ¼ cup (60 ml) of coconut milk at a time to reach a nice, pourable consistency.

* The freeze-dried strawberries really make this cake gorgeous and sets the flavor over the top, but if you don't have them, add an extra ½ cup (60 g) of powdered sugar and top the cake with some fresh raspberries or raspberry preserves.

* No food processor? No problem. Crush the freeze-dried strawberries until they are a fine powder and mix them with the sugar, rosewater, and milk in a bowl until completely combined.

PERFECT CHOCOLATE TORTE

I'm happy to say that this reliable, simple recipe always produces a delicious chocolate cake with a really thin, almost fragile exterior top crust. Folding in the whipped egg whites gives this a wonderful lightness that balances the rich fudge of the bittersweet chocolate.

This torte is great a couple of hours after baking it, but it really is even better after you refrigerate it overnight, or for a day. The addition of coconut oil, instead of the traditional butter, makes it a little sturdier after it's refrigerated.

If you are taking this kind-of-fancy snack cake to the next level, add Whipped Coconut Cream (page 230) and fresh berries. Or eat it on its own, wrapped in a piece of parchment paper, wherever you are.

YOU
DO **YOU**

MAKE THIS

❏ vegan

✗ dairy-free

✗ gluten-free

✗ traditional

YIELD

One 9-inch torte

Angela Says

✱ If you don't have two stand mixer bowls, carefully transfer your whipped egg whites to a clean glass or metal bowl. Clean the stand mixer bowl and use it to whip your egg yolks. Or you can whip the egg whites by hand using a clean glass or metal bowl and a whisk.

INGREDIENTS

Nonstick spray for pan

1⅓ cups (205 g) chopped bittersweet chocolate or chips, dairy-free if necessary

½ cup (120 ml) melted coconut oil

6 large eggs, separated

¾ cup (150 g) granulated sugar

½ cup (48 g) almond flour

1½ teaspoons sea salt

1 teaspoon pure vanilla extract

Preheat your oven to 350°F. Grease a 9-inch round cake pan with nonstick spray and line it with parchment paper.

Melt your chocolate and coconut oil together over low heat. At the bakery, I like to do this in a cake pan, popped into the preheating oven. But at home, you can put them together in a little saucepan and melt slowly over low heat. Once melted, and whisked together to be homogenous, just set the mixture aside while you whip up the eggs.

Place your egg whites in the bowl of a stand mixer fitted with the whisk attachment, or whisk them by hand using a whisk and a large glass or metal bowl. Whisk, starting on medium-low speed and increasing to high, until they are completely foamy, adding ½ cup (100 g) of the sugar. Continue to whisk until stiff peaks form. The peaks will stand up on their own, but will still be shiny and luscious looking. Set aside.

Combine the egg yolks and remaining ¼ cup (50 g) of the sugar in a clean stand mixer bowl and whisk vigorously until they are pale in color and very thick, about 5 minutes. The mixture will form ribbons on top of itself when you lift up the whisk over the bowl. Add the chocolate mixture and mix to incorporate. Then, add the almond flour, salt, and vanilla and mix again to incorporate.

Fold the whites into the chocolate mixture with a rubber spatula, starting with about one-quarter of the whites and incorporating them fully to lighten the chocolate mixture. Then, add the rest of the whites and gently fold all together until homogeneous but still fluffy.

Pour the batter into your prepared pan and pop into the oven. This is a recipe that performs best when you let the oven stay shut most of the time—if you are opening and closing the door, it can disrupt the rise of the egg whites and deflate your batter. When I tested this recipe at the bakery, I did have people opening and closing the oven a little and it still fared well, but I always recommend keeping the oven door closed as much as you can during baking.

Bake for about 50 minutes, or until the torte no longer jiggles when you gently tap the pan and it doesn't give too much when you press the middle.

Remove from the oven and let cool completely in the pan at room temperature. Store in the fridge overnight or for a day or two, until you are ready to eat it. I always add a sprinkle of powdered sugar and fresh berries, or Whipped Coconut Cream (page 230).

FROSTINGS
+ FILLINGS
+ EXTRAS

These are the finishing touches for most of the recipes in this book. I have given you pairing ideas throughout this book, but please feel free to mix and match! Sometimes I feel like having a batch of Classic Vanilla Buttercream (page 223) around just to use for dipping my cinnamon roll or any extra cookies laying around. You'll find that these are the perfect final flourishes for your showstopping, delicious treats—and the perfect last-minute addition to your more casual sweet snacks.

CLASSIC VANILLA GLAZE

Glaze is subjective.

I went through a phase at Goldenrod and at home where I really wanted a picture-perfect bun. To me, this meant that I waited until the buns or cakes were completely cool to glaze with a super-thick powdered sugar and milk glaze. I wanted an opaque glaze that sat really lusciously and heavily on top of each bun. This kind of glaze is very photogenic and very delicious.

A few years after Goldenrod opened, I started glazing treats while they were still hot, with a thinner glaze than I had used previously. This meant the glaze melted into the dough and into the crevices of spiced sugar and fine cake crumb.

THICK GLAZE

This gives you a thick, opaque glaze for buns and cakes for a totally picturesque finish.

YIELD

1 cup glaze

INGREDIENTS

2½ cups (300 g) powdered sugar

2 tablespoons milk, almond milk, or your favorite nondairy milk, plus more as needed

1 teaspoon pure vanilla extract

Whisk together the ingredients in a medium bowl until smooth, adding additional liquid if too thick. Use this glaze on cooled items.

THIN GLAZE

We use this at Goldenrod when our buns come right out of the oven, letting it seep into all of the swirls and crevices of the dough.

YIELD

1 cup glaze

INGREDIENTS

2½ cups (300 g) powdered sugar

¼ cup (60 ml) milk, almond milk, or your favorite nondairy milk (we prefer almond), plus more as needed

½ teaspoon pure vanilla extract

Whisk together the ingredients in a medium bowl until smooth, adding additional liquid as needed. Use this glaze on hot items for a glossy, translucent finish.

CLASSIC VANILLA BUTTERCREAM + VARIATIONS

YOU
DO YOU

MAKE THIS

✗ vegan
✗ dairy-free
✗ gluten-free
✗ traditional

This is a very simple buttercream. I tried desperately when I switched to a dairy-free diet to find a butter replacement that had a clean taste and could be used in buttercream without dramatically altering the texture or taste. One day, I hesitantly tried vegetable shortening in my buttercream recipe, and it was absolutely delicious. I try to keep some on hand just in case I want to dip into it with a cookie or a cake scrap.

If you can eat butter and love butter, feel free to use it in this recipe instead of the shortening.

YIELD

4 cups buttercream, enough for one 8-inch cake

INGREDIENTS

- ¾ pound (3 sticks, 338 g) unsalted butter, at room temperature, or 1½ cups (288 g) vegetable shortening

- 5½ cups (660 g) powdered sugar

- ½ cup (120 ml) milk, almond milk, or your favorite nondairy milk (we prefer almond)

- 1 tablespoon pure vanilla extract

Combine your choice of fat and the powdered sugar in the bowl of a stand mixer fitted with the paddle attachment. Start the mixer on the lowest speed and mix for about 30 seconds to disperse the fat in the sugar. Slowly stream in the milk and vanilla. Once all the ingredients have been added and are incorporated, increase the mixer speed to high and let the buttercream whip for 3 to 5 minutes. I love fluffy buttercream. Use immediately, or transfer to an airtight container. This can be stored at room temperature for 24 hours. Transfer to the refrigerator and store for up to 1 week.

Angela Says

* Use buttercream as a filling for a cookie sandwich. Favorite combinations include chocolate chip with coffee, peanut butter with vanilla or chocolate, chocolate with peanut butter, the sky's the limit!

BUTTERCREAM VARIATIONS

Follow the same method and storing instructions for all the buttercream variations as listed for Classic Vanilla Buttercream:

DARK CHOCOLATE

¾ pound (3 sticks, 338 g) unsalted butter, at room temperature, or 1½ cups (288 g) vegetable shortening

5 cups (600 g) powdered sugar

½ cup (45 g) unsweetened cocoa powder

½ cup (120 ml) milk, almond milk, or your favorite nondairy milk

1 tablespoon pure vanilla extract

2 teaspoons brewed coffee (optional)

STRAWBERRY

¾ pound (3 sticks, 338 g) unsalted butter, at room temperature, or 1½ cups (288 g) vegetable shortening

5 cups (600 g) powdered sugar

½ cup (30 g) freeze-dried strawberries, crushed

½ cup (120 ml) milk, almond milk, or your favorite nondairy milk

1 tablespoon pure vanilla extract

Pink gel food coloring, as desired

ALMOND

¾ pound (3 sticks, 338 g) unsalted butter, at room temperature, or 1½ cups (288 g) vegetable shortening)

5 cups (600 g) powdered sugar

½ cup (120 ml) milk, almond milk, or your favorite nondairy milk

1 teaspoon almond extract

BITTER COFFEE

¾ pound (3 sticks, 338 g) unsalted butter, at room temperature, or 1½ (288 g) cups vegetable shortening

5½ cups (660 g) powdered sugar

3 tablespoons instant coffee powder

⅓ cup (80 ml) milk, almond milk, or your favorite nondairy milk

1 tablespoon pure vanilla extract

LEMON

¾ pound (3 sticks, 338 g) unsalted butter, at room temperature, or 1½ cups (288 g) vegetable shortening

5½ cups (660 g) powdered sugar

¼ cup (60 ml) milk, almond milk, or your favorite nondairy milk

¼ cup (60 ml) fresh lemon juice

1 tablespoon pure vanilla extract

Yellow gel food coloring, as desired

CINNAMON

¾ pound (3 sticks, 338 g) unsalted butter, at room temperature, or 1½ cups (288 g) vegetable shortening

5½ cups (660 g) powdered sugar

¼ cup (60 ml) milk, almond milk, or your favorite nondairy milk

2 teaspoons ground cinnamon

1 tablespoon pure vanilla extract

YOU
DO YOU

MAKE THIS

☐ vegan

✗ dairy-free

✗ gluten-free

✗ traditional

MARSHMALLOW SWISS MERINGUE

I tend to eat this straight from the bowl. Or dip cookies into it. Or use it to frost cakes. It's heavenly. Light as air and perfect for frosting cakes and topping pies.

YIELD

4 cups meringue

INGREDIENTS

4 large egg whites

1¼ cups (250 g) granulated sugar

½ teaspoon sea salt

You are going to cook the egg whites and sugar in a heatproof bowl set over a pot of boiling water—so be sure to choose a pot that accommodates resting a bowl on its rim. Put your egg whites, sugar, and salt into your bowl and place over the pot of boiling water. Whisk constantly for 8 to 10 minutes, until the egg whites reach a temperature of 175°F. If you don't have a candy thermometer, feel free to test the old-fashioned way: insert a clean knuckle in the mixture quickly. It should be very hot to the touch.

Transfer to the bowl of a stand mixer fitted with the whisk attachment and mix on high speed for about 10 minutes, or until the bowl is cool to the touch and your meringue has formed stiff peaks.

Angela Says

※ I love this meringue because it super light and fluffy and perfect for using as a dairy-free frosting for cakes and cup-cakes. You can also bake this as beautiful fluffy meringues. Preheat your oven to 200°F and line a baking sheet with parchment paper. Add gel food coloring and freeze-dried fruit powder to the meringue as desired! Make piles of meringue on the prepared sheet and bake for 2 hours. Enjoy immediately or store in airtight containers for up to 2 days.

SWISS MERINGUE BUTTERCREAM

This is your fancy, luscious, buttery buttercream. Some occasions just call for it! This is the buttercream that we use for all wedding cakes that don't need to be dairy-free. It provides great structure, has a beautiful shiny finish, and travels well when cold.

YIELD

5 cups buttercream

INGREDIENTS

5 large egg whites

1 cup (200 g) granulated sugar

½ teaspoon sea salt

1 pound (4 sticks, 454 g) unsalted butter

2 teaspoons pure vanilla extract

You are going to cook the egg whites and sugar in a heatproof bowl set over a pot of boiling water—so be sure to choose a pot that accommodates resting a bowl on its rim. Put your egg whites, sugar, and salt into your bowl and place over the pot of boiling water. Whisk constantly for 8 to 10 minutes, until the egg whites reach a temperature of 175°F. If you don't have a candy thermometer, feel free to test the old-fashioned way: insert a clean knuckle in the mixture quickly. It should be very hot to the touch.

Transfer to the bowl of a stand mixer fitted with the whisk attachment and mix on high speed for about 10 minutes, or until the bowl is cool to the touch and your meringue has formed stiff peaks. Add the butter, a few tablespoons at a time, until all the butter has been added. Add the vanilla and continue to whip the buttercream for about 5 minutes. Use immediately, or store in an airtight container in your refrigerator for up to 2 weeks.

Angela Says

✱ Cut your butter while the meringue is whipping. You'll want this ready to pop in the mixing bowl in pre-cut pieces when the time comes!

✱ I had a chef-instructor in pastry school who told us that it is nearly impossible to ruin this recipe. Your buttercream might look curdled for a few moments after adding the butter. That's fine! Just keep whipping it. This is not an easy or inexpensive recipe to make, so please don't give up on it if yours if it seems a little off. If you add very cold butter, it might curdle. Warm the bowl in some warm water or over the flame on your stove and start mixing again. If you add the butter before your meringue is fully cooled, the buttercream might be really thin. Pop the bowl in the fridge for about 20 minutes and start whipping again. You can always fix your buttercream!

WHIPPED COCONUT CREAM

This recipe marked a big change in how I perceived eating dairy-free. It gave me hope that I would find the same joy in nondairy treats that I had found in my past life of butter- and cream-filled treats. This whipped coconut cream is everything I wanted whipped heavy cream to be: it is super rich and luscious, sweet on its own without adding any sugar, and the perfect accompaniment to so many of my favorite desserts in this book.

YIELD

2 cups whipped coconut cream

INGREDIENTS

Two 15-ounce (425 g) cans full-fat coconut milk

2 teaspoons pure vanilla extract

Refrigerate the cans of coconut milk for at least 24 hours. Freezing doesn't work, so just be patient, plan ahead a little, and use the refrigerator.

After they have been refrigerated, open the cans and carefully scoop out the top layer of cold, solidified coconut milk into the bowl of a stand mixer fitted with the whisk attachment. Reserve the remaining milk for another use. Add the vanilla extract and mix on medium-high speed until most of the lumps of coconut fat have broken up and soft-peaks have formed, about 5 minutes. Refrigerate or use immediately.

Angela Says

✳ The most reliable brand of coconut milk that I have used for this recipe is the Whole Foods 365 brand full fat coconut cream. Try to choose a brand that doesn't add any gums or sweeteners to the milk, as the final product will be impacted by these additional ingredients.

CHOCOLATE OVEN GANACHE

Chocolate ganache is a melted mixture of chocolate and milk or cream that makes a really luscious way to finish a dessert. Traditionally, you heat the milk or cream just until it starts to simmer, then you pour it over a bowl of chopped chocolate. Whisking the two ingredients together gently gives you a perfectly melted chocolaty mixture.

Then, we made *oven ganache*. There was a time around the holidays when all four burners on our small stove were either taken or being used as pie storage, and every baker had about five projects going at once. The combination of all of this made it really hard for me to use the stove to heat the milk, and I couldn't be there to watch it heat up and not burn. So, I poured the milk in a cake pan with the amount of chocolate chips, and put the pan in the oven. A few minutes in the hot oven, and a quick few seconds of whisking, and I had the most beautiful, shiny ganache of my life.

We continue to use the oven ganache method at Goldenrod Pastries. It's very convenient when you have multiple projects on your hands and you don't have the freedom to watch milk warm up. If you do have that freedom, follow the first method I mentioned above. For everyone else, try oven ganache.

YIELD

3 cups ganache

INGREDIENTS

1¾ cups (420 ml) milk, almond milk, or your favorite nondairy milk

1½ cups (232 g) dark chocolate chips or chopped chocolate, vegan if necessary

½ teaspoon sea salt

2 teaspoons brewed coffee (optional)

Preheat the oven to 350°F.

Combine the chocolate chips and milk in an 8- or 9-inch round cake pan and pop it into the oven. Check on your ganache after 5 to 6 minutes. Mix gently with a whisk to combine. If the chocolate isn't melting easily, put the pan back in your hot oven for another 1 to 2 minutes. Once the chocolate and milk are fully melted and mixed together, add the salt and coffee (if using).

Use immediately or, if you are making this in advance, store in an airtight container and gently reheat on the stove or in the microwave, stirring constantly.

CARAMEL SAUCE

This is the recipe we use as the starting point for anything we want to do with caramel. I am notorious for making terrible caramel, and even I can make this. Caramel-making moves fast, though, so you want to make sure you have all of your ingredients and supplies ready to go when you get set up. This is a recipe that moves really slowly, until it's ready—then you need to move quickly to get it done. Be prepared, have no fear, and you'll do great!

This recipe can easily be scaled up or down—though I wouldn't recommend making a batch smaller than half of this quantity.

YIELD

2 cups caramel sauce

INGREDIENTS

- 2 cups (400 g) granulated sugar

- 2 cups (480 ml) milk, almond milk, or your favorite nondairy milk

Place all the sugar in a heavy-bottomed saucepan. Add about ½ cup of tap water to make the sugar the texture of wet sand right where it meets the ocean. Make sure there aren't any dry patches of sugar at the bottom of the pan. With a damp paper towel or pastry brush, wash down any sugar from the sides of the pan. Sugar that is on the sides of the pan can crystallize, and will then spread crystals to the caramel.

Place the pan over medium-high heat and leave it alone. Be sure your milk is measured, close by, and ready to be poured into the caramel. You don't want to stir the sugar, as it can cause crystallization. This recipe relies on your eye. You want your caramelized sugar to turn a dark amber color. Because you are adding an equal amount of milk to the caramel, you can let it go a little darker than you think. Once the pan starts to smoke a little, turn off the heat and carefully pour in the milk. Let the bubbles and steam settle down a little before you use a whisk to mix it all together.

Once the milk and caramel are well combined, set aside to cool in the pan. Pour into an airtight container and store in the fridge until you are ready to use this.

Angela Says

✳ Use this as a syrup to brush on such cakes as vanilla, chocolate, and carrot. It will make your cakes extra moist, while imparting a really incredible deep, dark caramel flavor.

✳ Use this recipe to make our favorite Sticky Pecan Buns (page 58).

✳ Reduce this to a temperature of 250°F to thicken and use as a caramel sauce for cakes, ice-cream sundaes, or as a filling for cakes and a topping to drizzle on cupcakes.

LEMON CURD

This lemon curd will put to rest any idea that lemon curd is difficult to make. The main skills you need are cracking eggs and whisking. You can do this! I like to add a gelatin sheet to the curd because it adds just a little extra stability to help the curd set up and stay nice and stable. This isn't totally necessary for you to use, but gelatin sheets have become easier to find in the last few years, and I give you all the info on how to use them in this recipe. Feel free to leave it out if you don't want to use them; your curd will just be a little less thick, which is totally okay with me, if it's okay with you!

YIELD

2 cups lemon curd

INGREDIENTS

1 gelatin sheet (optional)

1 cup (240 ml) fresh lemon juice

1 cup (200 g) granulated sugar

½ teaspoon sea salt

4 large eggs

4 large egg yolks

½ cup (120 ml) melted coconut oil

Place the gelatin sheet (if using) into a bowl of ice water and let it bloom while you make the rest of the curd.

Combine the lemon juice, sugar, salt, eggs, and egg yolks in a large heavy-bottomed pot. Whisk together vigorously before heating. Once the mixture is well mixed and homogeneous, place the pot over medium heat. Whisk constantly, being sure to reach the bottom and edges of the pot. After about 10 minutes, the mixture will be very thick and bubbly. Turn off the heat. Remove the gelatin sheet from the water and squeeze out any excess water. Add the coconut oil and gelatin sheet to the hot lemon curd mixture. Whisk to combine.

Set aside in the pot to cool at room temperature, whisking occasionally. Transfer to an airtight container to store in the refrigerator for up to 2 weeks.

FRUIT PRESERVES

Fruit preserves are a Goldenrod staple ingredient. We use them to fill The Original Crumble-Buns (page 64) and layer cakes, to put on top of cheesecakes, and with our favorite cookies, such as Coconut Berry Thumbprints (page 90). Once you have an idea of how preserves are made, and the technique behind them, these recipes will only be a guide.

Goldenrod's Rules for Preserves:

- The five basic ingredients are fruit, sugar, sea salt, fresh lemon juice, and starch, such as cornstarch. All fruits have varying water contents. This is important to know because the more water in the fruit you are using, the more starch you will need to thicken the preserves. Berries have a higher water content than apricots, so you will use more starch to thicken a berry preserve than an apricot preserve.

- All preserves start by cooking the fruit with sugar. This can be granulated sugar, brown sugar, honey, or maple syrup. Use the least amount of sugar possible so you don't dilute the fruit flavor.

- Once the sugar and fruit have cooked together and are a bubbly sauce, whisk together cornstarch and lemon juice, then add it to the hot fruit sauce. Whisk constantly until the mixture is thick and bubbly.

- Let cool completely before using.

Those are the basics! The following three recipes are for fruit preserves that have varying levels of water content. Berry preserves will use the most starch and peach preserves will use less starch to thicken. Apples have a high concentration of *pectin*, a thickening agent, so you won't need any starch to thicken apple preserves.

MIXED BERRY PRESERVES

Use fresh berries in the summer or when they're available to you, and use frozen berries when it's more convenient.

YIELD
3 cups preserves

INGREDIENTS

5 cups (500 g) mixed berries (I like a mix of strawberries, raspberries, and blackberries)

¾ cup (150 g) granulated sugar

½ teaspoon sea salt

½ cup (120 ml) fresh lemon juice

5 tablespoons cornstarch or tapioca starch

Combine the berries and sugar in a medium saucepan. Cook for about 15 minutes, or until the sauce is cooked together and bubbly, stirring often. Whisk together the salt, starch, and lemon juice in a small bowl, then add to the hot fruit sauce. Whisk constantly until the mixture is thick and bubbly. Remove from the heat and let cool completely before using.

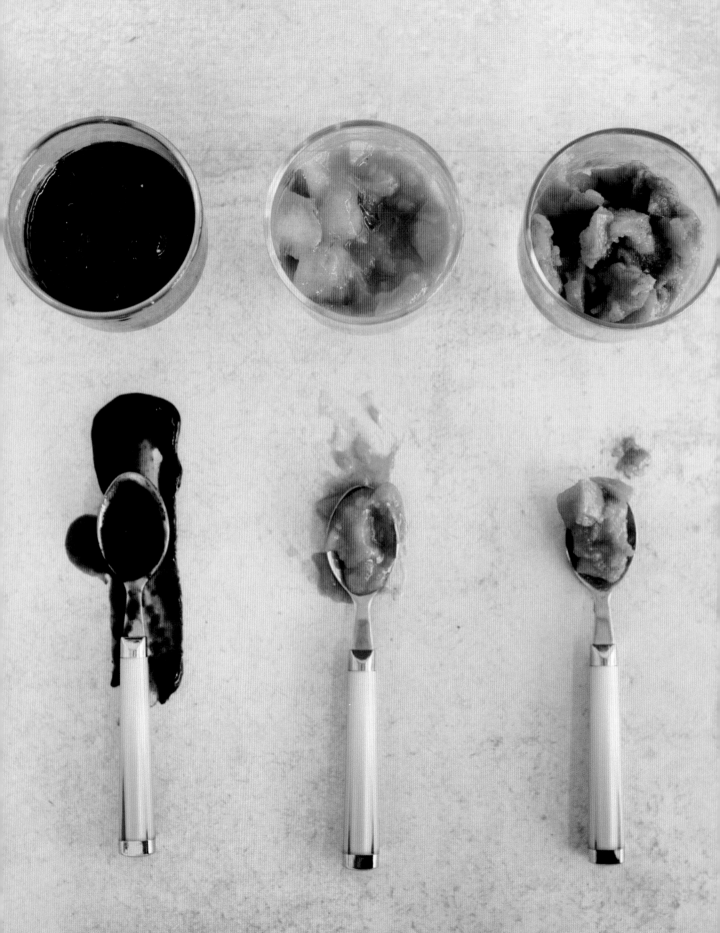

PEACH PRESERVES

Use fresh peaches when possible!

YIELD
3 cups preserves

INGREDIENTS

7 peaches, pitted and chopped into 1-inch pieces

½ cup (89 g) light brown sugar

½ teaspoon sea salt

½ cup (120 ml) fresh lemon juice

5 tablespoons cornstarch or tapioca starch

1 teaspoon ground turmeric

Combine the peaches and brown sugar in a medium saucepan. Cook for about 15 minutes, or until the sauce is cooked together and bubbly, stirring often. Whisk together the salt, starch, and lemon juice in a small bowl, then add to the hot fruit sauce. Whisk constantly until the mixture is thick and bubbly. Take the preserves off the heat and mix in the turmeric. Let cool completely before using.

APPLE PRESERVES

Our customers love The Original Crumble-Buns (page 64) with apple preserves maybe more than any other flavor. You can use peeled or unpeeled apples. I prefer to use unpeeled because it helps the fruit hold together and prevents the apple preserves from becoming applesauce.

YIELD
3½ cups preserves

INGREDIENTS

5 cups (750 g) apples that have been cored and chopped in 1-inch pieces (I love to use Granny Smith or Jonagold)

½ cup (89 g) light brown sugar

½ teaspoon sea salt

1 teaspoon ground cinnamon

1 teaspoon ground cardamom

1 tablespoon fresh lemon juice

Combine the apples, brown sugar, salt, cinnamon, cardamom, and lemon juice in a medium saucepan. Cook for about 30 minutes, or until the fruit is cooked and bubbly, stirring often. Let cool completely before using.

COOKING WITH SIGNIFICANT WOMEN
An Essay by My Mom, Mary Cariotto Garbacz

Learning to appreciate food, cooking, and hospitality began with women who were expected to provide sustenance for family and friends. Before long, their reputation was built on their abilities as cooks and hostesses.

The commonality of all of these mentors was patience. Each of these women taught me with kindness, whether I was a young girl or a new bride. I don't remember a single raised voice—only a focus on the goal of learning to be the next generation of cook and hostess.

Young girls were expected to learn to operate cooking appliances, prepare, and properly serve food as soon as they were able. My mother, Helen Dow Cariotto, was born in Nebraska in 1912. She told a story of the Spanish flu outbreak in 1918 that killed more than 675,000 people in America alone—scores of millions worldwide. She was the only one in her family of five who did not contract the flu, and at the age of six, she stoked the woodstove, lit the fire, and prepared hot chocolate for her bedridden parents and siblings.

The necessary frugality of people in even recent history has led to a respect for food and its preservation. I was born in 1953, eight years after the end of World War II and deep in the years of the Korean conflict. My father, Joseph Cariotto, was a colonel in the US Army and served away from home from 1941 to 1945. During those years, my grandmother, Cora Stevens Dow, lived with my mother in Lincoln, Nebraska, and together, they acquired food and preserved everything they could. They had lived through the Great Depression, so they were always afraid lean times would come again. They canned meats, fruits, and vegetables so nothing went to waste.

The 1950s and '60s were rich tutorials for me. Although I didn't realize it at the time, every kitchen I entered taught me a lesson of food preparation and hospitality that I use to this day.

Angela, pictured with Danielle, her sister-in-law, first employee, cake decorator extraordinaire, best friend.

I learned to slip the skins from bushels of ripe peaches and peel the yellow skins from bushels of pears by the time I was four years old. I stood on a kitchen chair at the counter with a paring knife, sharing the job of preparing the fruit with my mother and grandmother. There was a warm camaraderie in the kitchen that went beyond the heat of the summer and the fires on the gas stove. We stood there in aprons my grandmother had made, perspiring and working on the piles of quickly ripening fruit. My mother made a light syrup to pour over the fruit halves packed into the dozens of quart canning jars. She then processed the jars in a boiling water bath. Our family enjoyed these fruits every winter. My mother probably remembered the difficult, hot work in a kitchen without air-conditioning, but the rest of the family just enjoyed the fruit!

My father was the son of poor, Sicilian immigrants. Joseph was determined to live a better life, so he and my mother created a family life in which every meal contained each of the four food groups—protein, dairy, bread, and fruit and vegetable. My job, from about the age of three, was to set the dinner table precisely, then make a relish plate containing carrot strips, Italian olives, and slices of provolone cheese cut from a giant ball that hung from a rope in the Italian grocery store. The relish plate was served in a sectioned crystal tray every single night. Meanwhile, my mother prepared the nightly meal of salad, roast beef, chicken or pork, vegetables, and potatoes, with fruit and a cookie for dessert. The salad preparation followed my father's preference for iceberg lettuce (really the only lettuce commercially available at that time), other crisp vegetables when available, and tossed with a capful of corn oil and apple cider vinegar and seasoned with salt, pepper, and a spoonful of sugar. Each individual salad was served with a pepperoncini pepper or two. After watching my mother prepare the salad, I often asked to prepare it. Mom also was an outstanding hostess; anyone was welcome at our table. Her holiday meals were inspired, memorable, plentiful, and beautifully prepared. It was from her that I learned that the hard physical work of food preparation was rewarded with good memories, good friends, and good health.

My mother's sister, Irene Dow Milldyke, prepared magnificent and innovative savory dishes. Her husband, John, kept a large garden every summer and she found many ways to use its bounty. Summer lettuces became "wilted lettuce" under her artful touch. A little bacon, onion, cider vinegar, and a bit of sugar boiling in a skillet became the dressing for a mound of fresh lettuces. Freshly dug new potatoes tasted like cream under her skilled hands. Chicken, fried with a crisp outside and a moist, done inside, was a special treat. Chicken-fried steak with mashed potatoes and gravy in Irene's kitchen was unlike anything I've tasted since.

Aunt Irene's daughter-in-law, Doris Evans Milldyke, also is an excellent cook and hostess. Born in a small town in the Nebraska Sandhills, Doris also learned to cook from an early age, but refined her food preparation skills when she and her husband and daughters lived in England. It was from her that I learned further lessons of entertaining, including the preparation and serving of fancy appetizers and beverages.

My father's sister, Providence Cariotto Zarvos, lived in Lincoln and spent a career as a cook for employees of a local watch factory. She often invited our family to her home for a Sunday dinner that began with tossed salad, then mostaccioli pasta, meatballs, and marinara sauce, served with homemade rolls. After we were already full from the salad and pasta, her husband, Nick, would bring in platters of T-bone steaks, fresh off the grill. As if that weren't enough, apple dessert with a sweet, oaty topping came out to finish the meal.

It was from Aunt Providence that I learned about Italian hospitality, which means more food than anyone could possibly eat. That lesson has stayed with me throughout my decades in the kitchen.

My husband's mother, Katarzyna Pawęska Garbacz, immigrated to the United States in 1949 with her husband and two daughters. My husband, Stan, is the only member of his family to be born in the United States. Katarzyna was taken from her home at age 14 when the Nazis invaded Poland in 1939. She and other young girls were loaded into a boxcar and taken to Germany to be slave laborers until the US Army liberated them at the end of World War II in 1945. Baba, as we called her, described herself as a "plain cook." Quite the contrary. Her cooking was a fusion of Polish and German cooking, melded with lessons she learned when she came to the United States. Her roast beef and potatoes with dill gravy melted in your mouth. Her yeast rolls, knotted just so and topped with an egg wash and poppy seeds, were a work of art and so delicious that you'd quickly find that you'd eaten three of them, with her favorite butter. She used that same yeast dough to make the base for a peach coffee cake, topped with a butter-sugar-flour-vanilla crumb she called *krucinski*, then baked it to golden perfection. A jelly-roll pan of warm peach coffee cake, along with a gallon of milk, awaited our family whenever we returned from a trip. Within 30 minutes, at least half of both had been consumed while we stood in the kitchen.

Today, I have a collection of recipes, cookware, bakeware, and serving ware. Some traveled to my kitchen from these women, such as Aunt Providence's sauce spoon and Baba's yellow Pyrex mixing bowl.

ACKNOWLEDGMENTS

I love the life and energy that I feel every day at Goldenrod Pastries, and every day I bake. I knew that conveying that energy and the story of Goldenrod, and my absolute love and obsession with eating and making pastries, would be one of the biggest challenges with this book. Daniel Muller has been my photographer since the very first Goldenrod photo shoot in 2014. Our styles have evolved both as individual artists and when we come together on photo shoots. I am in awe of the photography that Daniel created for this book. I feel like he gave our readers a chance to peek inside Goldenrod Pastries, but also to experience how special these recipes are. Daniel: I cannot imagine working with anyone else on this book. Thank you for your creativity, for reading my mind, for adding your own touches, and for never settling for a shot that just wasn't exactly perfect. Thank you for working through the sweltering summer shoots in our bakery photo studio, and for always being eager to keep trying new things with our shoots. You are a friend and a true professional.

My marketing, photography, style, and true hustler Goldenrod girl, Maggie. Thank you for spending months researching props, making mood boards, and making some of the very key design decisions that makes this book so beautiful. You became my confidant and one of my biggest cheerleaders through this whole process, always being a sounding board and never leaving a photo shoot until the last dish was done and the last prop was packed away. All during your third trimester of pregnancy, during one of the hottest summers imaginable! THANK YOU.

My bakers at Goldenrod who helped prep for almost every photo shoot, taking on more work for themselves in order to help me. Amber, thank you for showing up in the early mornings of those shoots to make buns, decorate cookies, bake pies, and for offering the moral support and companionship I needed at the time. I have loved watching you grow as a baker.

Danielle, my sister-in-law, pastry chef extraordinaire, and Goldenrod's very first employee. You get my brain like very few people do. You are the most fun

247

person I have ever baked with. I love watching you work and I never know what will happen next.

My manager, Natalie, for taking on additional responsibilities while I worked on this book. You are one of the most hard-working and trustworthy people I have ever met.

To the Goldensquad, thank you for your dedication to this bakery. You show me what it means to support people close to you when they need it the most. It wasn't until my time working with all of you that I felt like I could truly be myself. Thank you for providing that environment for me, and to our customers. I love you all so very much.

Thank you to my mom, Mary, who spent hours and hours poring over the pages of my manuscript, finding every spelling error, inconsistency, and deleting all of my superfluous commas. Thank you for sending me to grade school with a slice of blueberry pie in my hand for the walk to school and for letting me have red velvet cake for breakfast. Thank you for letting me help you in the kitchen, especially when I know I was just getting in your way. Thank you for your tireless hours making us food and providing us the opportunity to share conversation around the dinner table and around a mixing bowl full of chocolate chip cookie dough, all while working a full-time job.

To my dad, Stan, for being the example of a gentleman and a strong man, but with the softest heart of anyone I've ever met. You have shown people all over the world what it means to create honest relationships, especially through your Donut Diplomacy. I'll never forget when I told you I wanted to move away to make a difference in a new place and you calmly told me that if I wanted to make a difference, there was plenty for me to do right here in Lincoln, Nebraska.

Andy and Betsy, I loved our late-night sibling cookie parties growing up and I miss them so much. I hope Lucy and Sebastian grow up eating as many cookies and cakes as we did!

My husband, Russell. The person who encouraged me to fly to San Francisco for a blogging workshop two months after we got married, helped me look for a place to build my bakery, and who drops whatever he's doing to run to the store for us or to make a delivery. Your dinners have sustained me through the busiest moments of running this business. Thank you for loving what I do, supporting what I do, and never acting surprised when I'm ready to start my next adventure.

Rebecca Forsyth, my friend and hairstylist. Thank you for being on set to make sure every curl was in place, to reapply lipstick every time I ate a bite of cake, and for always helping me talk through my roadblocks during this process.

To all of my girlfriends who have called me, fed me, and listened to me go on and on about the bakery and this cookbook for years. Women make my world go 'round. You make the world a better place for me. I love you all so much. You know who you are.

GOLDENROD COMMUNITY: THANK YOU!

To my PR teams at Carrie Bachman Public Relations and Bolster Media, my agent Sally Ekus of the Lisa Ekus Group, and to my editor, Ann Treistman, and the team at The Countryman Press. Thank you for believing in me; teaching me more about writing and making a cookbook than I ever thought possible; and for giving me a platform to tell the story of Goldenrod Pastries and the world that we've created in the Great Plains. You helped make one of my biggest dreams come true.

INDEX

*Italics indicate illustrations.